**Research & Education Association**

New
SAT 2005:
Inside Out!

David Benjamin Gruenbaum

Founder, Ahead of the Class
A private education and test prep company
Irvine, California

Research & Education Association, Inc.
61 Ethel Road West
Piscataway, New Jersey 08854

www.rea.com

New SAT 2005: Inside Out!

Printed in the United States of America

Library of Congress Control Number 2004090113

International Standard Book Number 0-7386-0039-3

REA® is a registered trademark of Research & Education Association, Inc.

Research & Education Association, Inc.
61 Ethel Road West
Piscataway, New Jersey 08854

E-mail: info@rea.com
Website: www.rea.com

To Heather: my wife, my reason.

Contents

Contents

CHAPTER 2

Writing   53

Contents

CHAPTER 3

Critical Reading   121

CHAPTER 4

Math   175

Contents

CHAPTER 5

Conclusion   253

Foreword

For those of us in the SAT world, 2001 was a strange time. At the beginning of the year, the president of the University of California (UC) system made a startling announcement proclaiming his desire to drop the SAT I as a requirement for UC applicants, and at the same time touting the virtues of the SAT II Subject Tests. This statement was particularly important because the UC system is arguably the most powerful public university system in the United States.

To be frank, I was completely astonished. For many years, the University of California system had required the SAT I and three SAT II subject tests for admissions decisions. Could the UC system actually be considering requiring as its only admissions exam requirements the three SAT II subject tests, a battery of tests not even used by the vast majority of colleges in the country? Then came a completely new thunderbolt: Not only was the University of California considering moving to only using the SAT II for admissions, but there was now talk of changing to a "Five SAT II" plan. In other words, the UC system was considering a more confusing plan: requiring applicants to take *five*, instead of three, SAT II subject tests.

The more I thought about this plan, the more concerned I became. If the University of California picked its own set of tests, what was to stop every other college in the country from picking completely different sets of tests, thereby creating chaos for college applicants?

Everyone knows that across the country, students have been overburdened with testing. In addition to college admissions tests, there are state tests, national tests, AP tests, etc. As I considered the problem of overtesting, something started brewing in my mind. Throughout all of the years I have helped students prepare for the SAT, one thing has always bothered me. Students work with me to prepare for the SAT I, which is a math and English exam, and then they come back to me to work on the SAT II, which also covers math and English, and sometimes these same students even return to work with me on the ACT, which is also a math and English test. Why do there have to be so many tests of math and English?

Sometime in August 2001, a new idea hit me. Why couldn't there be a single test of math and English? Why couldn't the SAT I and SAT II be merged into a single test?

On September 9th, 2001, I wrote a letter to Gaston Caperton, the president of the College Board, suggesting that the College Board create a new SAT. Then I went to work on the University of California system and the media. In October 2001 I spoke before the UC Board of Regents to present my idea and over the next few months I wrote columns for many newspapers pushing the idea of a new SAT.

At first I received all kinds of resistance, especially from members of the University of California system. I was certain I had failed, and that the UC system was going to segregate from the rest of the colleges in the country with some sort of weird augmented SAT II plan. But in January 2002, I received news that was elating. The UC system had changed course and was now asking for a new test. Much of the language in the UC statement echoed what I had been asking for.

As they say, the rest is history. The College Board agreed to create a new SAT for the entire country and here we are.

I hope that you enjoy this book. It is truly the work of thousands of authors, the students I've personally helped prepare for the SAT I, SAT II, and ACT over the last sixteen years.

I want to clarify that the purpose of this book is to present a *preview* of the New SAT. Over the last year, I have answered thousands of questions concerning the New SAT, ranging from the normal—such as "Will the New SAT have an essay?"—to the bizarre—"Is it true that all colleges are going to stop using the SAT?" Even though the New SAT will not be first administered until March 2005, parents and students alike are already curious and apprehensive.

The presentation of this book may seem quite foreign to many of you. I know some of you are accustomed to the standard style of most test preparation books: Memorize a few thousand words, memorize a hundred math formulas, here's a bunch of tricks to help you "beat the test," etc. That is not the style that I use in my SAT preparation classes and it is not the style of this book. Instead, you will find that this book is shorter and simpler than most other SAT preparation books. I teach simple logic and to improve SAT scores is to integrate education and humor.

There are several people I need to thank. First of all, I want to thank my wife, Heather. Heather's help in finishing this book has been incalculable. Whether she was helping me sift through ideas, spending countless hours proofreading, or just supporting me when I felt I couldn't see the end, Heather was the *reason* I finished this book. I also want to thank my parents, Michael and Thelma Gruenbaum, and my brothers, Peter and Leon Gruenbaum, who were also invaluable in proofreading the book. I also wish to express my gratitude to both Rafael Magallán and Wayne Camara of the College Board. I have always been impressed with their eagerness to hear my ideas and their continual desire to improve the SAT. In addition, I want to thank the book's wonderful illustrator, Jimmy Chau. Jimmy truly helped bring *The Incapables* to life.

Now I would like to speak of the wonderful team at REA, Inc. I want to thank Dr. Max Fogiel, the founder and president emeritus of REA, and Carl Fuchs, the president of REA, for having the courage to take on a completely new breed of education book. In addition, I would like to thank John Paul Cording for his great work in creating a vital new dimension of the book on the Internet, and I also want to thank Pam Weston and her production team, Christine Saul at REA and Nick Pellegrino at Network Typesetting, Inc., for their wonderful work in graphic arts design and typesetting, respectively.

Finally, I would like to thank my editor, Larry B. Kling, for his contribution to this book. Larry's commitment to even the smaller details of the book, his constant equanimity, his patience, and his unrelenting assistance in helping me bring to life my vision were all remarkable.

For those of you taking the New SAT, have a good time with this book. In fact, knock yourself "wooscious." (Don't worry, I will explain this word soon enough.)

David Benjamin Gruenbaum

About Our Author

David Benjamin Gruenbaum has worked with thousands of students, helping them to prepare for tests like the SAT I, SAT II, and the ACT. With his wife, Heather, David co-owns *Ahead of the Class*, a private education company. REA's *New SAT 2005: Inside Out!* is David's second book. In 1991, David and Fred Joblin co-authored a radical vocabulary book, *Word Up*.

David and Heather make their home in Irvine, California. Readers can e-mail David by visiting **www.REA.com/SAT**.

About Our Contributors

Heather Chagnon Gruenbaum authored the essay "Westfield: Small Town Joys." She also wrote the essay "Charlayne Hunter-Gault: A Study in Activism," which was adapted from a 2001 research paper titled *Women in the Civil Rights Movement: The Discourse of Black Female Activism.*

Milt Cohen edited the mathematics material.

Terry Casey of INKandLINE indexed the book, and **Diane Goldschmidt** and **Gianfranco Origliato** of REA proofread it.

REA's **Christine Saul** designed the book and **Jeff LoBalbo** coordinated pre-press electronic-file mapping.

> **Readers should recognize that following publication of this book, changes can occur in the New SAT's format, content, and testing schedule. REA will include new information and updates about the New SAT at www.REA.com/SAT.**

Introducing...
The Incapables

This book is set in an imaginary classroom. The students in the class have earned the nickname *The Incapables*. If you have any question as to why this class is named *The Incapables*, don't worry. After just a few pages of reading, you will understand.

Each of *The Incapables* has a distinct personality, with accents and phrasing to match. If you find yourself mouthing out loud what the characters are saying, don't panic; you're not crazy. In fact, this sort of behavior is perfectly normal. If you would like to know more about the characters, go to REA.com.

Without further ado, let's meet *The Incapables*.

Thor, The Surfer Dude

Thor is the typical Southern California surfer. When he speaks, Thor has the California voice quake: "Du-hude, well awl roight!" Thor wants to know if you're allowed to take the SAT outside so he can work on his "mondo" tan. Thor even makes up his own words and language: Look for "wooscious" and the way he uses "very" later in the book. Even though Thor seems like a sunbaked moron, he actually is quite a good reader.

Xasmine, Shopper Girl
(pronounced "Jasmine")

Xasmine is the consummate shopper girl. Her name is pronounced "Jasmine." If you're wondering why she spells her name with an X, as Xasmine says, "Like, it was so my parents' idea. My mom and dad were all, 'Let's be original,' and besides they didn't have spellcheckers back then." When the Critical Reading section is discussed, Xasmine wonders, "Oh…my…God… Is the reading going to die?" Even though Xasmine seems like a ditz, she actually is quite strong in math.

Uhhhhh, The Jock
(pronounced "Uhhhhh")

Uhhhhh is the ultimate jock. He often cannot pronounce the letter "t" and says things like "dis" and "dat." His language skills are so poor that he is beyond illiterate; he is **illingual**. Unlike the other students, who may be strong in math, writing, or reading, Uhhhhh even struggles with the name of the test. "What's da AST?" he asks. Uhhhhh's best hope for doing well on the New SAT is to have someone else take the test for him.

Wictoria, Witch-in-Training

Wictoria is a teenager who is obsessed with witches. Everything Wictoria thinks about, speaks about, and writes about involves witches. For example, when Wictoria is asked "What is the greatest problem facing the world today?" she says, "Many people feel that war or poverty is the greatest difficulty, but has anyone stopped to think how hard it is to find a good broomstick these days?" Instead of normal teenage problems like acne and boyfriends, Wictoria is more concerned about "the advantages of boiling newts versus steaming them." Even though she is weak at math and reading, Wictoria is a strong writer.

Zino, The Foreigner from Where?
(pronounced Zee-no)

Zino is an immigrant, but no one knows where he comes from. His accent switches constantly and he has a great deal of trouble speaking, reading, and writing English. He is constantly screwing up American phrases; for example, instead of saying "That's cool," he says, "That's freezing." Zino aces all of the SAT II foreign language exams but he has taken the SAT 25 times and still hasn't gotten a good score.

Uboreme,
The Strange One
(pronounced "You bore me")

Uboreme is one of those strange types who is negative about everything. Instead of filling in the multiple-choice answers on the test, Uboreme writes his own answers. We don't know what Uboreme's strengths and weaknesses are because he walked out during the practice SAT to go to the bathroom and never returned.

**Dr. S. A. Tea,
the teacher**
(Dr. Samuel Aardvark Tea)

Dr. S. A. Tea is a highly trained SAT preparation specialist. His biggest problem is the six characters he's been assigned to teach.
Good luck, Dr. S. A. Tea!!!!

The New SAT: What's It All About?

The New SAT: What's It All About?

How this Book Works

If you haven't heard, the SAT is changing. The New SAT will first be administered in March 2005. The purpose of this book is to give you a preview of the new test and give you the confidence you need to do well on the test.

The first thing you will notice when you open this book is how short it is in comparison to other SAT books. In this time-crazy world, this is a good thing. Most people who write test preparation books have no idea what teenagers' schedules are like these days. You don't have time to read a 500- to 1000-page book.

So, be happy — this book is short! Most of you could easily read it in a week or less. The format of the book is also simple. There are five main areas:

1. An introductory area that covers general questions about the New SAT and also introduces you to the cartoon characters in the book

2. An area that discusses the new Writing section

3. An area that discusses the new Critical Reading section

4. An area that discusses the new Math section

5. A final area that tells you what you can do in the future to keep boosting your SAT score

Most of the areas have three components:

1. A dialogue between Dr. S. A. Tea (an SAT preparation instructor) and, shall we say, an "interesting" class of students, *The Incapables*. There are a lot of jokes. You're allowed to laugh.

2. Suggestions for handling different portions of the SAT. Unlike many other SAT preparation books, this book will only *suggest* different approaches to handling the New SAT. In the end, you should pick what works for you.

3. Practice Exercises

Before We Get Started

Throughout this book:

1. The *New SAT I* will simply be referred to as the *New SAT*

2. The outgoing *SAT I* will simply be referred to as the *Current SAT*

3. Unless they are specifically named, colleges and universities will be referred to as colleges

Destroying Some SAT and Education Myths

First, I would like to debunk some SAT and education myths.

<u>**Myth Number 1**</u>**: The SAT Is a Bad Test**

Several test-preparation companies have perpetuated this nonsense over the years. The truth is that the Current SAT is an incredible test of math and English, and the New SAT will be an incredible test of math and English. The College Board (the organization that owns the SAT) and ETS (Educational Testing Service, the company that designs the SAT questions) work very hard to make sure that the test is as fair and unbiased as can be. First, imagine how difficult it would be to create an exam that is a fair test of reading, vocabulary, and math. Then factor in constantly monitoring and changing the test to try to satisfy critics who complain that the test is biased in some way.

The SAT is a terrific test. It is biased against only one group: the uneducated.

<u>**Myth Number 2**</u>**: Studying for the SAT Doesn't Help You Beyond the SAT**

When I took the PSAT (Preliminary SAT) in high school, I had only a slightly above-average verbal score. Yet I was one of the best students in my school and I went to one of the best high schools in the United States. In addition, I was a voracious reader. How could I have gotten such a low verbal score?

The answer is simple: My vocabulary was horrible. Before I took the SAT, I worked with a list of 3,500 words and tried to learn as many of these words as possible. This started a lifelong interest in vocabulary for me.

Unlike school, where students can often get by with memorizing formulas for math or renting videos instead of reading books, the SAT actually forces every test taker to think. Students who spend time preparing for the New SAT will find that their writing, reading, and math skills will improve.

<u>Myth Number 3</u>: Education Can't Be Fun

Many students hate going to school. They can't wait until school is over to do something "fun." Why can't learning be fun and educational at the same time? The point is that learning **can** and should be fun and educational at the same time. I hope you find this book to be a testament to this theory.

Who Says You Can't Have Fun and Learn at the Same Time?

The typical boring SAT preparation book merely lists a lot of methods and has a gazillion practice problems. The goal of this book is for you to learn and have fun at the same time . . . Novel concept, eh?

Anyway, let's meet the New SAT!

Questions About the New SAT

Dr. S. A. Tea: Good morning, class. First let me introduce myself. My name is Doctor Samuel Aardvark Tea, but you can call me Dr. S. A. Tea.

Class: Good morning, Dr. S. A. Tea!

Dr. S. A. Tea: Okay, now does anyone know what SAT stands for?

Thor: That's Sooooo easy. Surfing and Tanning, roight, Du-hude?

Wictoria: Spells and Trolls?

Uhhhhh: What's da AST?

Dr. S. A. Tea: Well, I can see that I have a lot of work to do here. Actually, SAT used to stand for *Scholastic Aptitude Test* and, later, *Scholastic Assessment Test*. Because the new test measures both aptitude and knowledge, however, the initials *SAT* now no longer stand for anything in particular. The College Board (the people who own the SAT) continues to use the name SAT because it has such high name recognition. Are there any other questions?

Xasmine, *waving her hand:* Oooh, Dr. S. A. Tea, is it okay if I call you "El Doctor?" I'm all so the whiz at Español.

Dr. S. A. Tea: Sure (struggling to read the name), what's your name, X-as-mine?

Xasmine: Actually that's pronounced JASmine, El Doctor.

Dr. S. A. Tea: But, uh, Xasmine, how can you possibly pronounce an *X* as a *J*?

Xasmine: Like, it was so my parents' idea. My mom and dad were all "Let's be original," and besides they didn't have spellcheckers back then.

Dr. S. A. Tea: Okay, did you have a question?

Xasmine: So-oooh, can you take the test wherever you want to? Like, I was all talking to my friends and we were all, "Let's take the SAT at Beverly Hills so we can scope out all the rich, cute guys. Then after the test, like we could so-oooh go shopping on Rodeo Drive and . . ."

Dr. S. A. Tea*, cutting her off:* Yes, Xasmine, if you sign up early you can take the test any place that it's offered. HOWEVER, don't sign up late because sometimes the spaces fill up at the more popular test sites. Last year, there was a kid from Boston who had to take the test in Guam. Are there any other questions? Yes, Uboreme?

Uboreme: Why do we exist?

Dr. S. A. Tea: Okay. Well, clearly some of you are very strange. . . . Zino, you have a question?

Zino: Just-a-one, Dottore. When-a do we start a-learning how to meeta the women onna the Internet?

Dr. S. A. Tea: Actually, Zino, this is an <u>SAT</u> class. Okay, one final question . . . Thor?

Thor: Doctor Du-hude, lo-ike, can you take the SAT outside? You see I am working on this mondo tan . . .

Dr. S. A. Tea*, cutting him off:* First of all, for those of you who don't know, let's quickly break down the different college admissions tests:

What Are the Different Admissions Tests Required by Colleges?

1. CURRENT SAT or SAT I. The Current SAT is a verbal and math test. The name of the organization that owns the SAT is the College Board. In March 2005 there will be a New SAT.

Most colleges will likely accept either the New SAT or ACT.

2. ACT. The ACT is also a verbal and math test. The name of the organization that owns the ACT is ACT Inc. The ACT is also changing and the first ACT with the new format will be administered in February 2005.

3. SAT II. The SAT II is a series of subject tests. Some of the subjects are: Math, Literature, Biology, U.S. History, and a range of languages. The SAT II tests are also owned by the College Board.

Which Colleges Require Which Tests?

1. The majority of colleges require either the Current SAT or the ACT. The country is split between students who take the ACT and the SAT. Students from the East Coast and West Coast tend to take the SAT more, while students from the South and Midwest tend to take the ACT more. Because students from different areas are taking two different tests, the majority of colleges will accept either test. In addition, many colleges have developed conversion charts that compare the SAT scores directly to the ACT scores. Most of these colleges just take whichever score (SAT or ACT) is higher. Always make sure that the colleges you are interested in will accept either test.

2. Some top colleges also require the SAT II. Some examples are the Ivy League schools (Harvard, Yale, Dartmouth, etc.), other top-notch private colleges (Stanford, University of Chicago, Northwestern, etc.) and the University of California system (UC Berkeley, UCLA, UC Irvine, etc.).

Will Colleges Require the Same Tests in the Future?

1. Although it is not certain, it is very likely that the majority of colleges will require the New SAT or the ACT. Ultimately each college makes its own decision and some colleges may decide to require only the New SAT **or** the ACT. However, because students in different parts of the country take the ACT or the SAT, most colleges will probably continue to accept either test. It is also possible that some colleges may accept the scores from the Current SAT for students who are applying in the fall 2005. Check with the colleges you are interested in to see what their policies will be.

2. It is also quite likely that many of the colleges that have required the SAT II in the past will continue to require the SAT II in the future. Currently, the majority of colleges that require the SAT II ask applicants to take three separate SAT II subject tests. This may change for some colleges. For example, the University of California has already indicated that it will require only two SAT II subject tests for its application process for the freshman class of 2006. In the future, some colleges may follow suit and also lower their requirement to two SAT II subject tests. You should always check to find out which tests are required by the colleges you will be applying to.

When Is the First Time that the New SAT Will Be Administered?

Dr. S. A. Tea: Okay, the reason that all of you are here is to practice for the New SAT. Who knows when the first New SAT will be given?

Xasmine, *jumping up and waving her hand:* Ooh, ooh, El Doctor! I know!

Dr. S. A. Tea: Okay, Xasmine, when?

Xasmine: As soon as they give the old SAT for the last time. *(Sits down, obviously pleased with herself.)*

Dr. S. A. Tea: Xasmine, while this is true, I think people are more interested in a time period. **The first New SAT will be administered in the spring of 2005.**

Uhhhhh: 2005? Dat's next year!

Dr. S. A. Tea: Uhhhhh, your concept of time is truly breathtaking. Anyway, here's the schedule I suggest for students who are completing their junior year in June 2005.

What's the TSA?

Dr. S. A. Tea's Suggested Schedule for Students Who Are Finishing Their Junior Year in June 2005

1. SAT II in May 2004

2. Current SAT in June 2004

3. The New PSAT in October 2004

4. The ACT in February 2005

5. The New SAT in March 2005

Why Consider this Type of Testing Schedule?

1. SAT II, May 2004. It is a good idea to consider taking the SAT II in May 2004 for two reasons:

> • **First, many "highly selective" colleges (colleges that take a low percentage of applicants) currently require that students take some SAT II subject tests for their application processes.**
>
> • **Second, SAT II Writing and Math subject tests will give sophomores a sneak preview of some of the new sections that will be part of the New SAT I.**

2. Current SAT, June 2004. There is no PSAT offered in the spring. If you are a motivated student who would like to start getting a feel for the New SAT, it might be wise to consider taking the Current SAT in June. Many of the sections on the Current SAT will be part of the New SAT.

3. New PSAT, October 2004. What is the PSAT? For the most part the PSAT is merely a shorter version of the SAT. There are two reasons to consider taking the New PSAT in your junior year. First of all, it's a chance to really start getting a feel for the New SAT. Just like the New SAT, the New PSAT will have reading, writing, and math sections. There will be two principal differences between the New PSAT and the New SAT. The New PSAT will be shorter and the test will not have an essay. Another reason to take the New PSAT is that if you do exceptionally well, you may qualify for a National Merit Scholarship.

4. ACT, February 2005. The ACT and the New SAT are going to be more similar than in the past. There are two reasons to take the ACT in February 2005. First, most colleges will likely continue the trend of accepting the applicant's higher score (New SAT or ACT). So, if you do well on the ACT, you won't even have to take the New SAT. Second, even if you don't do well on the ACT, it is still a good opportunity to get some practice for the New SAT. (For example, even though the New PSAT will not have an essay, the ACT's new format will include an optional essay.)

5. **New SAT, March 2005.** Obviously you should take the New SAT as soon as it is available.

What Should Students Who Are Finishing Their Sophomore Year in 2005 Do?

1. There is no need to take any tests in spring 2004. If you would like to use this book or other practice books to get used to the question types on the New SAT, that would be great.

2. Take the New PSAT in October 2005.

3. Consider taking the SAT II in May or June 2005. Only some of the top colleges in the country require the SAT II. Check with the schools you are considering to find out if they will require the SAT II.

How Will the New SAT Be Scored?

Dr. S. A. Tea: Now, let's talk about how the New SAT will be scored. On the Current SAT, there are only two areas: Verbal and Math. On the New SAT, there will now be three different areas that will be tested: Writing, Reading, and Math. What's the highest score you can get in any one area?

Class, *in unison:* 800 points.

Dr. S. A. Tea: Very good. Now, on the Current SAT, 1600 is perfect (2 × 800). What would be perfect for the New SAT?

Uboreme: If we didn't have to take it?

2400 is perfect on the New SAT.

Dr. S. A. Tea: First of all, I'll tell the jokes here, babe. Second, on the New SAT, because there are now three areas: Math, Writing, and Critical Reading, a perfect score will now be 2400 (800 × 3). Now, let's go the other way: What would be the lowest score you could get in any one area?

Class, *in unison:* Zero?

Dr. S. A. Tea: No, actually the lowest score per section is 200 points. It's also known as writing your name. . . . Now I am going to put up a chart with the scores from the practice New SAT. Because the scores are now calculated on a 2400-point scale, the totals are going to look a little strange.

PRACTICE SAT RESULTS

Name	Writing	Reading	Math	Total
Wictoria	650	540	320	1510
Xasmine	310	350	760	1420
Thor	340	670	320	1330
The Guess Monkey	270	280	270	820
Uhhhhh	200	200	200	600

The GuessMonkey

Dr. S. A. Tea: As we can see, most of you are good at one category. Wictoria scored high in the Writing category, Xasmine aced the Math section, and Thor did very well on the Reading portion. Then, we come to Uhhhhh. Uhhhhh, on each of the sections you had a 200, and you ended up with a total of 600.

Uhhhhh: 600, dat's good, right?

Dr. S. A. Tea: Uhhhhh, let me explain it to you like this . . . If you look at the chart, you'll notice that I had a monkey take the test. The GuessMonkey earned his name because he is randomly guessing all the way through the test.

Uhhhhh: Dat's interesting, but what does dat have to do with me?

Thor, laughing: Uhhhhh, du-hude, you did worse than the GuessMonkey!

Dr. S. A. Tea: Now, Thor . . . that's not very nice. We didn't talk about your Math and Writing Scores, which were quite low . . . .

Thor: Doctor Du-hude, at least I beat the GuessMonkey!

Dr. S. A. Tea: Anyway, moving on, there are two people in the class we don't have starting scores for: Zino and Uboreme. Zino is new to the class, so that's his excuse. In the case of Uboreme, however, you walked out to use the bathroom during the beginning of the practice test and never came back! What happened?

Uboreme: I was approached by some folks from the planet Septicor. They wanted to have a chat with me.

Dr. S. A. Tea, to himself: I bet they did.

How Many Times Should You Take the New SAT?

Wictoria: Great Wizard of the SAT, I heard that you're not allowed to take the SAT more than two times.

Thor: Doctor Du-hude, awl roight, I heard that they start averaging your scores if you take it more than three times.

Zino: I've-a signed up to take the SAT twenty-five times.

(The whole class turns to look at Zino.)

Dr. S. A. Tea: Twenty-five times . . . Why?

Zino: Well, when I-a came to this country, they said that I shoulda go to college. To go too-a college, you gotta taka this test, the SAT. So I sign uppa for the test. They send me a paper that says the test gonna be given in Daytona Beach. So I go to Daytona Beach. I get to the beach and there's a-nobody there. But, it'sa nice sunny day, so I sit on the beach and play with the sand and watcha the seagulls . . .

Dr. S. A. Tea, *cutting him off:* Okay, okay! So, what happened the second time?

Zino: The second time, they send me a sheet of paper that says this time the test gonna be given in Miami Beach. So I go to a-Miami Beach. I get to the beach and there's a-nobody there. But, it'sa nice sunny day, so I . . .

Dr. S. A. Tea, *cutting him off:* Okay, okay! I think we get the point.

Zino: But then, I-a figure out, when they say Daytona Beach, they-a no mean the beach. They-a mean the city, Daytona Beach. . .

Dr. S. A. Tea: Ah, progress.

Zino: So the third time I go to taka the test, I get to the test site and there's just-a one problem . . .

Dr. S. A. Tea: What's that?

Zino: The test is inna English, and to tella the truth, back then I'm notta the master of English that I am-a today.

Dr. S. A. Tea, *to himself:* Clearly . . .

Thor: Du-hude! Wait a second. You've taken the test twenty-five times, roight?

Zino: That'sa right.

Thor: How old were you when you took the test the first time?

Zino, *shrugging his shoulders:* 'bout the same-a age as you, 17.

Thor, *thinking out loud:* 17 plus 25. Du-hude, lo-ike you must be 97.

Dr. S. A. Tea: Thor, you numerical numbskull, 25 plus 17 is 42.

Thor, *laughing:* Still, this du-hude's been taking the SAT for twenty-five years.

Uhhhhh: What's da TAS?

Dr. S. A. Tea's Tips for How Colleges May Use the New SAT:

Before we discuss how many times you should take the New SAT, let's first examine how colleges may use the New SAT in the future.

1. In the past, most colleges have taken the highest overall score from the Current SAT on a given day. This trend will likely continue with colleges taking the highest overall score from the New SAT on a given day. In other words, on the Current SAT, if the first time you took the test you scored a 1000 and the second time you took the test you scored a 1200, most colleges would just use the 1200. The same thing will most likely occur when the New SAT is put into effect.

2. In the past, a few colleges have taken the highest individual section scores from different days. For these few colleges this trend will likely continue as well. For example, on the Current SAT, if the first time you took the test you scored a 600 in Math and a 500 in Verbal, and the second time you took the test you scored a 550 in Math and a 580 in Verbal, some colleges would use the 600 in Math from the first time and the 580 in Verbal from the second time. These colleges would be taking the highest Math score from one day and the highest Verbal score from a different day. It is possible that these same colleges may do a similar thing with the New SAT. In other words, they would take the highest individual scores from all three sections: Math, Writing, and Reading, even if the highest scores occur on different days.

3. Since there are two Verbal sections and only one Math section on the New SAT, there is a possibility that some colleges may start doubling the math section. It is also pos-

sible that some colleges may double the math score for certain math-related majors (engineering, computer science, etc.). One source of major concern for colleges is the diminishing number of male applicants. It's an old cliché, but on average, boys still do seem to score higher on the Math sections while girls tend to score higher on the Verbal sections. If colleges double the Math section score, that may increase the amount of male students who are accepted.

4. There have been rumors for years that some colleges average the scores or limit the amount of times you can take the SAT. It is possible that there are some colleges that do average scores or limit the amount of times students can take the test, but I have never encountered a college that does this.

Dr. S. A. Tea's Tips for How Many Times You Should Take the New SAT:

1. First, attempt to familiarize yourself with the Current SAT average scores for the colleges you are most interested in attending. It is also important to see if you can discover separate average scores for Math and Verbal sections. For at least a year or so, many colleges will either post the average SAT scores or a range of SAT scores for the most recent freshman class. (Remember again that these are the **Current SAT** scores.) If you can find separate average scores for the Math and Verbal sections for the individual colleges you are considering, you may be able to make an estimate of what the average scores might be for the New SAT. Because there are two Verbal sections on the New SAT, it will probably be best to double the number from the Verbal section from the Old SAT and then add that to the Math section score of the Old SAT. Using this equation, you can get an approximation of what the averages for the New SAT score would be (based on your Current SAT score).

2. If you can't find separate average scores for the Math and Verbal sections of the Current SAT, multiply the overall average score by 1¹/₂. In other words, if a college only states that the average for the freshman class was about 1200, multiply that number by 1¹/₂. That would mean the average New SAT score for the freshman class at that college should be somewhere around 1800.

A COMPARISON OF CURRENT SAT SCORES WITH NEW SAT SCORES (New SAT score is Current SAT score multiplied by 1¹/₂)*

OLD SAT I	NEW SAT I
400	600
600	900
800	1200
1000	1500
1200	1800
1400	2100
1600	2400

(*This chart should only be used as a rough guide. If you want the most accurate way to compare the New SAT scores with the Current SAT scores, you should try to discover the separate average math and verbal scores for the colleges you are interested in; then you should double the verbal score and add the math score.)

3. Your initial goal is very simple: Try to beat the average SAT scores for the colleges you would like to attend. This is sometimes a difficult task because some colleges are deliberately vague with their numbers or may only use ranges. (In other words, a college might state that 50% of the freshman class scored between 500 and 600 on the Verbal section and 60% scored between 500 and 600 on the Math section.) Just do your best to try to estimate the averages.

4. Your final goal: Try for a great score on the New SAT. There is certainly nothing wrong with taking the New SAT two or three times. Maybe you'll be nervous one time, or maybe there will be a large number of math problems on one particular test that you can't solve. Since most colleges take the highest overall score there is no reason not to try to keep improving your score. Most importantly, though, some colleges are even rejecting students who score <u>above</u> the average SAT scores for their schools. In today's competitive college environment, it is difficult to know what SAT score is high enough. Contact the colleges you would like to apply to and ask what score they regard as good enough for admission to their schools.

Don't be afraid: Keep taking the SAT until you get the score you want.

How Important Is the SAT for the College Admissions Process?

1. For many colleges, SAT scores are an important part of the overall admissions decision. Many admissions officials rank the SAT scores as the second most important component of your record behind your GPA and schoolwork. But think about how much time students spend going to school and doing homework, and compare that to the amount of time most students spend on the SAT. Clearly, studying for the SAT is very important.

2. Colleges look at other factors besides GPA and SAT scores. Beating a college's average SAT scores does not mean that you are going to be accepted automatically. Many schools now consider leadership, volunteer work, and extracurricular activities when making admissions decisions.

New SAT Question Types

Conversation with Uboreme about the aliens from Septicor

Dr. S.A.Tea: So, Uboreme, tell me about the aliens from the planet Septicor.

Uboreme: They're short, round, and orange with black stripes.

Dr. S.A.Tea: Interesting... why did they pick you?

Uboreme: Actually, originally they picked Uhhhhh.

Dr. S.A.Tea: Really? Why did they change their minds?

Uboreme: Uhhhhh tried to dribble them.

Dr. S. A. Tea: Okay, class. When you took the practice New SAT, perhaps some of you noticed that there were some new sections that did not exist on the Current SAT. Who spotted something new on the test?

Xasmine: El Doctor, El Doctor, like, oh my god, there was all of these borrrring reading sections.

Dr. S. A. Tea: Yes, the College Board has added some new short reading-comprehension passages and eliminated the Analogy section.

Zino: There vas dis writing bissness.

Dr. S. A. Tea: Right, the College Board has also added a new Writing section to the New SAT. This section consists of an essay and a few different multiple-choice question types that test grammar.

Uboreme: Besides the aliens, the other reason I left the test was because there was all of these difficult math problems.

Dr. S. A. Tea: Yes, the College Board has also added some Algebra II math problems.

Uhhhhh: I had a lotta problems with the questions, like what should I do when I see a yellow light or when dere's an amublance coming up from behind you?

Dr. S. A. Tea: What's an amublance? Oh, _ambu_lance. . . . Uhhhhh, we're talking about the SAT, not your driving test!

Uhhhhh: I spent a lotta time preparing for da test — you mean that I studied da wrong thing?

Dr. S. A. Tea, *to himself:* All of your life . . .

What Are the New Question Types on the New SAT?

1. Three multiple-choice grammar question types (Identifying Sentence Errors, Improving Sentences, and Improving Paragraphs). These question types are the same as those on the multiple-choice grammar section on the SAT II and the old PSAT.

2. An essay. Unlike the other question types, the essay will be graded by readers.

3. Short reading passages. The College Board has not made a final decision about all of the new passages; however, according to the College Board Web site (www.collegeboard.com), the New SAT will " . . . include new shorter reading passages, with paragraphs about 100 words long . . . ."

What's New on the Math Section?

Some math questions from Algebra II. The Current SAT does not test concepts from Algebra II, however the New SAT will include some Algebra II questions.

What Sections Will Be Eliminated on the New SAT?

Goodbye, Analogies!

1. The Analogies section: The verbal section in which you were asked to compare two words and find a similar relationship in the answers.

2. The Quantitative Comparison section: The math section in which you were asked to compare two columns, Column A and Column B, and decide which quantity was greater.

What Will Be the Format of the New SAT?

According to the College Board, here is the latest proposed time format:

Critical Reading: 70 minutes total (two 25-minute sections and one 20-minute section)

Math Section: 70 minutes total (two 25-minute sections and one 20-minute section)

Writing Section: 50 minutes total (one 25-minute essay and one 25-minute multiple-choice section)

Variable Section: 25 minutes total (This is an area of the SAT where the test makers try out new questions and question types. It doesn't count toward the SAT score.)

This all adds up to over $3\frac{1}{2}$ HOURS OF TESTING!

Five Keys to Improvement on the New SAT

Your five keys to improvement on the New SAT are: **1. Self-Motivation and Practice, 2. Understanding the Test, 3. Building Your Brain, 4. Last-Minute Preparation and Attitude,** and **5. Focus**. Now let's take them one at a time:

#1. Self-Motivation and Practice

Obviously, self-motivation and practice are two crucial elements in changing your SAT score.

Dr. S. A. Tea: Let's now talk about practicing. Uhhhhh, how many hours a day do you practice sports, like basketball, weightlifting, running, etc.?

Uhhhhh: Da coach has us practice for four hours each day after school. Den I go to the weight room for an hour and sometimes I run for an hour after dat.

Dr. S. A. Tea: So, let's say during the week you are practicing six hours a day.

Uhhhhh: Okay.

Dr. S. A. Tea: And when did you start playing sports?

Uhhhhh: When I was three.

Dr. S. A. Tea: Uhhhhh, I just want you to think about this. Imagine if instead of playing sports six hours a day for the last 12 years, you had spent six hours a day studying for the SAT. Maybe we'd be having a conversation like this:

**(Imaginary conversation between
Dr. S. A. Tea and an intelligent Uhhhhh)**

Dr. S. A. Tea: So, Uhhhhh, congratulations! You got a 2390 on the New SAT. The only reason you didn't get a perfect score was you missed one question on the Sentence-Completion section.

Uhhhhh: Tres true, Samuel Aardvark — however, I am disputing that one question because I felt that "pejorative" was just as valid a response as the so-called right answer, "malevolent."

Dr. S. A. Tea: Wow, Uhhhhh. I can see your point.

Uhhhhh: By the way, what is this "Uhhhhh" business? You must really work on this guttural verbal habit. Next thing you know you'll be stuttering, old man. You couldn't possibly be referring to me by a childish nickname, could you? If so, please call me by my proper name, Horatio, in the future.

Dr. S. A. Tea: Uhhhhh, gee, Uhhhhh I don't know what to say . . .

Uhhhhh, *cutting him off:* Sorry, old man, I've got to run. I'm off to debate club. Today we'll be discussing the future implications of human cloning . . .

(Back to reality)

Dr. S. A. Tea, *to himself:* Instead we're having a conversation like this . . .

Dr. S. A. Tea: Uhhhhh, I'm not saying that you need to spend six hours a day studying for the SAT. I just want you to think about it. Imagine what your score could be if you even practiced a few minutes each day for the SAT.

Uhhhhh: What's da ATS?

Dr. S. A. Tea's Tips for Self-Motivation and Practice

1. Set college goals for yourself. Think about which colleges you would like to attend. Get to know their old average SAT scores so you can estimate what you need to score on the New SAT to have a good chance of admission.

2. Set numerical goals for yourself. On the Old SAT, students used to say, "I want to get a 1200" or "I want to get a 1400." On the New SAT, you might hear students saying things like, "I want to get an 1800" or "I want to get a 2100." (Sounds funny with the new numbers, doesn't it?) Use the scale on page 30 to pick a number that you want to aim for.

3. Use this book for practice and to identify your weaknesses. For example, if you are strong in math, perhaps you should work more on your reading and writing skills. At the end of this book the conclusion will suggest different books and materials you can use for practice to strengthen your weaknesses.

The more you practice, the higher your score will be.

#2. Understanding the Test

The SAT is unlike any other test that you have ever taken. It is crucial to understand as much as possible about how the SAT works. For example, what subjects are covered on the New SAT? When should you be guessing? How do the tricks work on the test? These are all important questions that you need to understand in order to feel comfortable with the SAT.

What subjects are covered on the New SAT?

Zino: I don't understand zis SAT? Vere is ze German test? Vere is ze French test?

Xasmine: Who cares about French? Who cares about German? What about the shopping test? I could ace a test on sales at Bloomingdale's!

Dr. S. A. Tea's Tip: Get to Know What's Actually on the New SAT

1. Use this book to get a feel for what subjects the New SAT will cover. As we have discussed, the New SAT is divided into three sections: Math, Writing, and Critical Reading. These three sections are further divided into different question types. For example, the Math section has both multiple-choice questions and a question type called *Student-Produced Responses*. By practicing with this book now, you will gain an overall sense of the new test.

2. Keep up with any new changes by going to REA.com. REA will provide the latest news on the New SAT at our Web site, REA.com.

When should you be guessing?

Wictoria: Great Wizard of the SAT, I never know when I should guess and when I should leave something blank.

Thor: I heard you shouldn't guess unless you can eliminate two answers.

Xasmine: I heard that you shouldn't guess unless you can eliminate three answers.

Conversation with Xasmine about mall:female ratio

Xasmine: El Doctor, what's the mall:female ratio at NYU (New York University)?

Dr. S.A.Tea: Don't you mean the male:female ratio?

Xasmine: Like, so duh. Who cares about men? If I go to NYU I want to know that I can go shopping!

Uhhhhh: I heart dat you shouldn't guess unless you can elim . . . elim . . . uh — get rid of five answers.

Dr. S. A. Tea: Uhhhhh! There <u>are</u> only five answers!

Dr. S. A. Tea's Tips for Guessing

1. As long as you can eliminate any answer, you should be guessing. You may have heard that there is a penalty when you mark something wrong on the Current SAT. While this is true (for all sections except for the essay and the Student-Produced Responses, a math question type), the point is that you only lose a fraction of a point. <u>The crucial thing to realize is that when you get an answer right, you are gaining a whole point</u>. Of course, the College Board could change its system for the New SAT, but that is very unlikely. Don't be afraid to guess. This book will teach you how to guess more intelligently, and the points you will pick up from intelligent guessing are crucial if you want to have a good score on the New SAT.

2. Don't panic if some of your guesses are wrong. Even if you get one out of four guesses right, you are gaining points on the SAT.

What about the tricks?

Xasmine: El Doctor, El Doctor! I heard that the mean old nasty test makers put all of these so-ooh horrible tricks on the test.

Dr. S. A. Tea: Yes, there are tricks on the Current SAT and there will certainly be tricks on the New SAT. In this book, you will learn how to recognize and avoid the tricks on the test.

Conversation with Zino about the tricks on the test

Dr. S.A.Tea: Let's talk about tricks on the test. First of all, who can spot the trick answer on this question?

Zino: (raising his hand) I can. The trick answer issa "F."

Dr. S.A.Tea: There are no "F" answers on the SAT.

Zino: Thatsa why it's such a good trick.

Dr. S. A. Tea's Tips for Handling the Tricks on the New SAT

1. If you're answering a difficult question, and you have truly solved the problem, go for it. When you know the right answer to a question, don't worry about tricks.

2. If you can't solve a difficult question, be careful of falling for a trick. On the difficult questions, the answers that seem to be obvious are often wrong.

3. Instead of obsessing about how the SAT shouldn't have tricks, learn how to spot the tricks. Hey, life is full of tricks. The SAT is doing you a favor.

If you know an answer, go for it. Don't worry about the tricks.

#3. Building Your Brain

*Let's be frank, unfortunately much of your school life now revolves around three things: memorization, constriction, and machines. The problem is that the SAT **and** life revolve largely around your ability to think: to use logic and common sense. If you want to get a great score on the SAT, it is crucial to improve your reasoning and logic ability.*

Memorization

Dr. S. A. Tea: Thor, describe to the class how you learn vocabulary for school.

Thor: Doctor Du-hude, that's muy simple. I take the list of words and I memorize them the night before the test.

Dr. S. A. Tea: Okay, and what happens after the test?

Thor, *laughing and looking around for support:* Du-hude, I forget them. I mean, what would be the point of remembering them? The test is ohhhhver.

Dr. S. A. Tea: What about math and history?

Thor: The night before the math test I very well memorize the formulas for math, and the night before the history exam I very well memorize the history dates for the history exam.

Dr. S. A. Tea: And after those tests?

Thor: I forget everything I memorized. It's just like what we talked about with the vocabulary. The test is ohhhhver.

Dr. S. A. Tea: So, in other words you spend all of this time memorizing and you haven't learned anything permanent.

Thor: Come on, Doctor Du-hude, how could I be learning anything permanent? This is school.

Dr. S. A. Tea: Thor, what if I told you that all the things you love, like TV, could help you remember vocabulary words and solve math problems.

Thor: Doctor Du-hude, that would be awwwwwwwwesome!

Zino: Yea, Dr. Dud, zat vould be freezing.

Dr. S. A. Tea: Huh?

Thor, *sighing:* I'll translate. Zino is trying to say, "That would be cool."

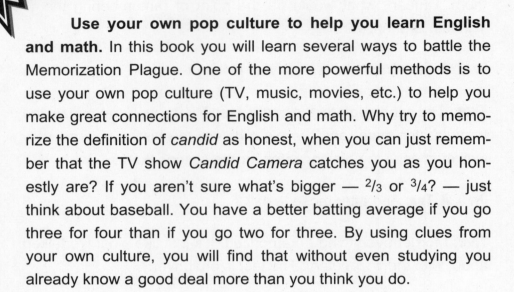

Dr. S. A. Tea's Tip: Learn, Don't Memorize

Break the school habit: Learn, don't memorize.

Use your own pop culture to help you learn English and math. In this book you will learn several ways to battle the Memorization Plague. One of the more powerful methods is to use your own pop culture (TV, music, movies, etc.) to help you make great connections for English and math. Why try to memorize the definition of *candid* as honest, when you can just remember that the TV show *Candid Camera* catches you as you honestly are? If you aren't sure what's bigger — $2/3$ or $3/4$? — just think about baseball. You have a better batting average if you go three for four than if you go two for three. By using clues from your own culture, you will find that without even studying you already know a good deal more than you think you do.

Constriction

Dr. S. A. Tea: Uboreme, why do you hate school so much?

Uboreme: It's limiting. The teachers only teach me one way to do everything and when I try to use my own methods, they don't give me any credit for my work.

Dr. S. A. Tea: Uboreme, the SAT is your dream test. You can use any method you want, no matter how weird, as long as you get the answer right.

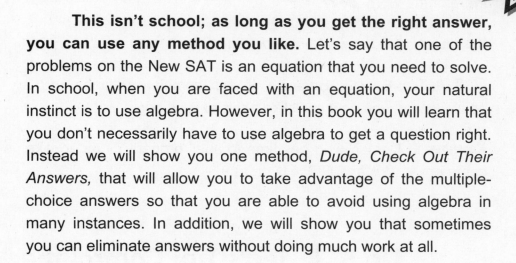

Dr. S. A. Tea's Tip: Breaking the Grip of the Constrictor

This isn't school; as long as you get the right answer, you can use any method you like. Let's say that one of the problems on the New SAT is an equation that you need to solve. In school, when you are faced with an equation, your natural instinct is to use algebra. However, in this book you will learn that you don't necessarily have to use algebra to get a question right. Instead we will show you one method, *Dude, Check Out Their Answers,* that will allow you to take advantage of the multiple-choice answers so that you are able to avoid using algebra in many instances. In addition, we will show you that sometimes you can eliminate answers without doing much work at all.

Throughout this book, you will learn how to look at questions from new perspectives that will allow you to handle even difficult questions.

Machines

Dr. S. A. Tea: Xasmine, when you write an essay at home, what's the first thing you do when you're done?

Xasmine: El Doctor, the spellchecker, duh-uh!

Dr. S. A. Tea: Then what do you do after the spellchecker has highlighted the words.

Xasmine: El Doctor, so duh! I punch in all of the changes as fast as I can.

Dr. S. A. Tea: Xasmine, I read one of your papers you wrote in class when you couldn't use a spellchecker and you used the word "theer."

So, like I so like this guy . . .

Xasmine: Yeah, so?

Dr. S. A. Tea: That word doesn't exist. Did you mean the word *there* or the word *their*?

Xasmine: I don't know. What's the difference?

Dr. S. A. Tea: Exactly. Because of your complete reliance on the spellchecker, you now spell like a dyslexic gibbon.

Xasmine: El Doctor, who has time to spell properly? I mean, like, come on . . . *Will and Grace* is on at 9.

Dr. S. A. Tea's Tip: Control the Machines, Don't Let Them Control You

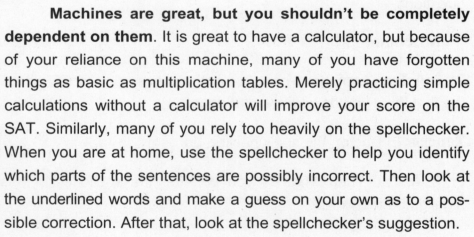

Machines are great, but you shouldn't be completely dependent on them. It is great to have a calculator, but because of your reliance on this machine, many of you have forgotten things as basic as multiplication tables. Merely practicing simple calculations without a calculator will improve your score on the SAT. Similarly, many of you rely too heavily on the spellchecker. When you are at home, use the spellchecker to help you identify which parts of the sentences are possibly incorrect. Then look at the underlined words and make a guess on your own as to a possible correction. After that, look at the spellchecker's suggestion.

#4. Last-Minute Preparation and Attitude

Last-minute preparation and your attitude play a huge part in determining your success on the SAT.

Dr. S. A. Tea: Okay, now it's time to be frank. How many of you went out the night before you took the practice SAT?

Xasmine, *waving her hand:* I did. There was an all-night rave in Hollywood. It was the world!

Uboreme: I don't sleep.

The SAT's a plot. Go on strike, man!

Dr. S. A. Tea: You mean *sometimes*, right?

Uboreme: Ever.

Uhhhhh: Went out . . . You mean, like for the team?

Dr. S. A. Tea: Clearly, catching up on your sleep is crucial. (*Then . . . looking at Uhhhhh*) Although for some of you, catching up with evolution might be more important. If you take the test when you're tired, instead of going to Harvard, you might find yourself attending a fine institution like Wombat Community College.

Zino: A Vombat is zom zort of furree animal, ja?

Dr. S. A. Tea: Right, Zino.

Thor: Ohhhhh, I get it. Wombat Community College . . . That's another funny one, Doctor Du-hude . . .

Dr. S. A. Tea: Three days later, but not to worry.

Wictoria: I was worried that I would be tired for the practice test, so I went to sleep last month.

Dr. S. A. Tea: Last month? Wictoria, you did look a little bit out of it during the test.

Thor: Doctor Du-hude, a little bit out of it? Wictoria was looking wooscious!

Dr. S. A. Tea: I ask, being very afraid of the answer: What is "wooscious"?

Thor: Doctor Du-hude, you got to get on the scene. "Wooscious" is halfway between woozy and unconscious.

Dr. S. A. Tea: Wooscious, huh. Well, I think Thor is right. I was watching you, Wictoria. When you took the practice test you were "ComaChick."

Thor: ComaChick, Doctor . . . Du-hude. That's another funny one, but it's not as funny as "wooscious."

Tip

Dr. S. A. Tea's Tips for Last-Minute Preparation and Attitude

1. Get a good night's sleep. Many high school students are only averaging five to six hours of sleep each night. Clear everything out the few nights before you take the SAT so that you can relax.

2. Eat a good breakfast. If you normally have cereal and fruit for breakfast, this is not the morning to discover meat.

3. Pump yourself up to take the test. Just think: If you have a good day, you might never have to take the SAT again.

If you don't do well on the SAT, don't worry. Take it again!

#5. Focus

If you're like most high school students, you're probably already sick to death of the word focus. *You have heard this word a thousand times before, not because of school, but because of sports. Focus is not just important for sports; it is obviously equally important for intellectual tasks.*

Dr. S. A. Tea: Class, what do you think your greatest problem is with this test?

Xasmine: There are those really hard things with all the letters in them.

Dr. S. A. Tea: Ah, you mean words. Anything else?

Wictoria: They keep asking me these silly questions with numbers in them.

Dr. S. A. Tea: Also known in the human world as math. . . . Anything else?

Uhhhhh: What was da question?

Dr. S. A. Tea: Exactly! For most of you, your greatest problem with this test is focusing.

Dr. S. A. Tea: Here's a chart of the focus level for each of you during this test:

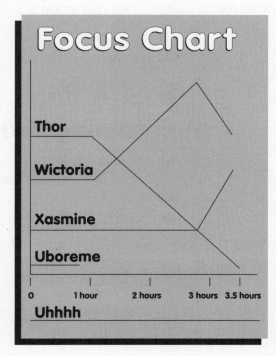

Dr. S. A. Tea: If we look at the chart, Thor starts high and ends low. Wictoria starts in the middle, then goes higher and ends low. Xasmine starts down low and actually improves her score by the end of the test. Then, as we discussed, Uboreme simply ups and leaves the test within just a few minutes. And, finally we have Uhhhhh, who isn't even on the chart.

(Rim shot)

Focus now and maybe you won't have to take the SAT again.

Dr. S. A. Tea: How many of you lost focus during the practice test?

(All hands in the class go up)

Dr. S. A. Tea: It is hard to focus on this test. Let me put it to you this way. If I had a movie of everything you were thinking about during this test, I wouldn't want to watch it. *(Rim shot)* But, think of it this way. Wictoria and Thor, if you could maintain the level you have at the beginning, and Xasmine, if you could snap in right away, and Uhhhhh, if we could get you ON the chart . . . think how much better all of your scores would be!

Dr. S. A. Tea's Tips for Maintaining Your Focus

The keys to maintaining focus are very similar to the keys for self-motivation and practice.

1. Try to beat the average SAT scores for the colleges you want to attend.

2. Set numerical goals for yourself. "I want to get an 1800," or "I want to get a 2100," etc.

Thor's Tip for Acing the New SAT: Dude, Check Out Their Answers

*Er. . . . Excuse me. Well, awl roight, could I have everyone's attention . . . Du-hude, this is **Thor**. Dr. Du-hude, er . . . Dr. S. A. Tea has asked me to introduce a cruuu-cial method that will help you to do gnarly on the SAT. One moment, du-hude. . . . Yes? (Thor has a brief conversation with Dr. S. A. Tea.)*

Okay, I'm back. I guess that Dr. S. A. Tea wants me to drop the surfer's accent so that all of you can understand what I'm saying. Lame! Anyway, here are my tips for using the method called Dude, Check Out Their Answers:

1. When you do multiple-choice questions, one of the five answers is right. Why not check out their answers?

Let's look at a sample from a reading passage:

> The farmers would spend days on end contemplating the
> **Line** future of the wheat industry. Because of the economy it was
> **30** often difficult to predict how much wheat they should grow in
> a given year and how they should market their product.
> There would be three years when the farmers couldn't pro-
> duce enough wheat and then they would have to endure a
> stretch when they could only sell their product at a loss.

Let's say that you were asked this question:

In line 34, the word "stretch" most nearly means

A) spread out

B) expand

C) period

D) magnification

E) crane

Sure, you could try to read around the word *stretch* for context, but wouldn't it be easier just to substitute in the test makers' answers to see which one fits the best. By "checking out their answers," you can clearly see that answer (C) works the best.

" . . . they would have to endure a **period** when they could only sell their product at a loss."

2. The Dude, Check Out Their Answers method also works for other sections on the test.

Let's look at a math problem:

The width of a rectangle is three times the length. If the perimeter of the rectangle is 32, what is the length?

A) 4   B) 5   C) 6   D) 8   E) 12

Now for most of you, your first inclination is to use algebra. In fact, in this case you could just make an algebraic equation to solve the problem. However, the *Dude, Check Out Their Answers* method may be a simpler way to approach the problem.

Let's start with answer (C). First of all, the question asks you to determine the length of the rectangle. If you assume that 6 is the right answer and you substitute in 6 for the length, everything else has to make sense in the problem for this to be the right answer. In other words, in this case the width would be three times the length, or 18.

However, 2(6) + 2(18) = 48 and we were looking for a perimeter of 32, as the problem states. This means that answer (C) is wrong. Clearly, we need to move down to an answer with a lower number. If you try answer (B), you will see that this answer will not work as well.

Now, let's look at answer (A). If you substitute in 4 for the length, then the width will be 12.

2(4) + 2(12) = 32

This is what we were looking for. **Therefore answer (A) is the right answer.**

(Looking behind him) Du-hude, it's **Thor** again. I think Dr. Du-hude has disappeared, so I am just going to say this in my own way. Don't forget to use the **Du-hude, Check Out Their Answers** method, Du-hude, awl roight!

Why wait? Start practicing now.

Why Start Practicing Now?

The New SAT won't be given until March 2005. That seems like a long way off. Why would you want to start practicing now?

The point is that even though a few things are still being finessed for the New SAT (for example, the exact amount of questions per section), we already know most of the important information for the new test. Also, since the New SAT will largely be a merger of the Current SAT I and Current SAT II Math and SAT II Writing tests, we have a good deal of samples to work from.

So, be smart. Start practicing now. Calculate pi to the three hundredth place, write a 200 page essay on the plight of man, read every book on this planet! Whip yourself into a New SAT frenzy!!!! Whoopee, Yee-Ha! Oops, sorry. Got a bit out of hand. Anyway, do yourself a favor: Start studying now.

YOU'RE DONE!

Congratulations! You have now finished the introductory area of the book. Next up, the Writing section. . . .

Writing

2

The Writing section is the largest addition to the New SAT. This section will be very similar to the kind of material one finds on the SAT II Writing test.

The Writing section on the New SAT will consist of two parts:

- **A 25-minute essay**

- **A 25-minute multiple-choice grammar section**

(Recently the College Board has released some documents stating the possibility that it might increase the essay length to 30 minutes. If the essay length is increased to 30 minutes, don't worry. The advice in this book for a 25-minute essay is almost identical to the advice for a 30-minute essay.) The New SAT will feature three different question types on the multiple-choice grammar section — the same question types that are currently featured on the SAT II Writing test and the PSAT. The three multiple-choice grammar question types will be:

- **Identifying Sentence Errors**

- **Improving Sentences**

- **Improving Paragraphs**

Because the Writing section is the largest addition to the New SAT, it has attracted the most public attention. Don't worry. It's easy to improve your Writing score.

The Permanent Effect of Improving Your Writing

Let's forget the SAT for a minute. Why is it important to improve your writing and grammar skills?

1. Improving your writing ability can change your grades in high school. Essay writing is obviously very important for subjects like history and English. The more you practice your writing, the stronger your essays will become.

2. Improving your writing ability can change your grades in college. In just a few years you will be in college and you will likely be writing many essays. Maybe in high school you can get away with essays that have sloppy structure, grammar, spelling, etc. Your college professors, however, are guaranteed to hold you to a high standard.

3. Improving your writing ability can even change the way you speak. Imagine if you had a great vocabulary and could phrase everything in a smooth and interesting manner. It's quite simple: the better you write, the better you speak. This would completely change the way other people viewed you, which in turn could change your social life and improve your career possibilities.

The Essay

Dr. S. A. Tea: Let's look at the work each of you did on the first essay. Here is the topic (prompt) of the first essay:

Topic: Can one day make a difference in someone's life?

Dr. S. A. Tea: We'll start with Wictoria, who had the highest score. Wictoria, you have a tremendous vocabulary, your phrasing and grammatical skills are quite good, but there is a big problem with your work. I think that this problem will become quite evident when we look at even just the beginning of your essay. Your first sentence reads:

> *"The world changed for me on the day that I received a letter from Salem, Massachusetts, informing me that I had been accepted by NCOYA (National Coven of Young Americans)."*

Dr. S. A. Tea, *continuing:* You then go on to discuss the advantages of boiling newts versus steaming them. The topic for a previous essay was, "Fear: is it a positive force or a negative force?" The first lines of your essay on this topic were:

> *"The world of the Wiccan is filled with strong emotions. These emotions help us to focus our power."*

Dr. S. A. Tea, *continuing*: The topic for the essay before was, "What is the greatest problem facing the world today?" The opening lines of your essay read:

> *"The world has many problems. Many people feel that war or poverty is the greatest difficulty, but has anyone stopped to think how hard it is to find a good broomstick these days?"*

Dr. S. A. Tea, *continuing*: Wictoria, can you see a pattern here?

Wictoria: Yes, I can. I start all of my essays with the phrase, "The world."

Dr. S. A. Tea: No! No! <u>All</u> of your essays are about witches. I am open-minded, but do you realize that most of the essay readers are going to think that you are seriously wacked? All you have to do is write about something quasi-normal and you will be all set. Now, let's move on to Thor's essay. Thor, you have an unusual start to your essay. The top of your paper seems to be all wet.

Thor: Doctor Du-hude. Awl Roight. That is sooooo easy to explain. You see, loike I was writing about surfing and I'm quoight afraid I spilled my Slurpee. I was going to wipe it up, but then I thought, no-oh way Du-hude . . . if I'm talking about surfing and the paper's wet, that's going to be a gnarly visual!

Dr. S. A. Tea: Thor, the essay grader said that the paper completely fell apart in her hands! She had to tape it back together. Now let's look at your introduction as a response to the prompt, "What was the best day of my life?" You wrote:

> *"It was a sunny day and I was amped. Previously I had been axed, but then I hit an aerial and I was carving . . . it was the world."*

Dr. S. A. Tea, *continuing:* Thor, can you see that outside of your little world of pre-melanoma shark chew that no normal human could possibly understand those sentences?

Thor: Shark chew. That's another funny one, Doctor Du-hude.

Dr. S. A. Tea: Then we come to Xasmine. Xasmine, when it comes to writing, you also seem to have a firm grasp on the important things in life. Your introduction reads:

> *"It was a beautiful day:) My mom was all like, 'Let's go to Nordstrom.' Brandy, I just have to talk to you later."*

Dr. S. A. Tea, *continuing*: Is it just me, or is there anyone in this class who can follow what Xasmine is saying?

Xasmine: El Doctor, like that totally makes sense. It so does! It was a beautiful day and I was happy, so I put in the smilie. Then I thought to myself, like maybe the essay readers will be all like, "Oh, wow. Does this girl value her family?" So I brought in my mom, but here's the coolest part . . . I tied it to my favorite activity in the world: shopping. Then I remembered, Oh, my God. I just have to tell Brandy about how I saw Tom yesterday.

(Sound of a phone ringing.)

Xasmine, *answering her cell phone:* Helloooo? Brandeeeeeee . . . I was just talking about you!

Dr. S. A. Tea: Next, we come to Uboreme. Your first sentence reads:

> *"Just remember . . . I am ALWAYS watching you."*

Dr. S. A. Tea, *continuing:* Clearly, this is probably not the best topic to choose. Also, Uboreme, I have been commanded to give you this.

Uboreme: What is it?

Dr. S. A. Tea: It's a restraining order to keep away from the person who graded your essay. He's a bit worried. Next we move on to Uhhhhh. Uhhhhh, your paper starts,

> *"Te gratest day my lif was wen we won the lige champagneship.*

Dr. S. A. Tea: Uhhhhh, I just don't know where to begin. To be frank, you could have written a better paper by randomly choosing words and punctuation. What can I say to someone who misspells the word "the"? Finally, we come to Zino. Zino, here's what you submitted for your essay:

> *Milk*
> *Bread*
> *Orange Juice*
> *Lettuce*
> *Lean Ground Beef*

Dr. S. A. Tea: Zino, what is this?

Zino: So sorry, Maestro, I theenk I gave you my grocery leest.

Dr. S. A. Tea: So, class, I think we need to start at the beginning. Let's start with some of the rules of the essay.

How Long is the Essay and How is It Graded?

1. Collegeboard.com, the official College Board Web site, states that the time allotted for the essay on the New SAT will be 25 minutes. As I mentioned in the beginning of this chapter, there is

a chance that the essay time will be lengthened to 30 minutes. Again, the advice for a 25-minute essay and a 30-minute essay is almost identical.

2. Each essay is graded on a scale of 1-6 (6 is the highest score, 1 is the lowest). Two readers score each essay and the total essay score is the sum of the two readers' scores (i.e., 2-12). If the two readers' scores differ by more than two points, a third reader is brought in to help determine the score.

What the College Board Says About Grading the Essays

An essay with a score of 6 (the highest score):

An essay in this category is *outstanding*, demonstrating *clear and consistent mastery*, although it may have a few minor errors. A typical "6" essay achieves the following:

- **Effectively and insightfully develops a point of view on the topic and demonstrates outstanding critical thinking, using clearly appropriate examples, reasons, and other evidence to support its position**

- **Is well organized and clearly focused, demonstrating clear coherence and smooth progression of ideas**

- **Exhibits skillful use of language, using a varied, accurate, and apt vocabulary**

- **Demonstrates meaningful variety in sentence structure**

- **Is free of most errors in grammar, usage, and mechanics**

Conversation with Uhhhhh about the difference between an essay and the SAT

Dr. S.A.Tea: Now, there's one more point I'd like to make about the essay...

Uhhhhh (cutting him off): Doctor, you are wrong.

Dr. S.A.Tea: Speak up, Uhhhhh. This is a major moment for you. You're actually challenging a thought.

Uhhhhh: You keep sayin' "SA," not "SAT." You're leavin' out da "T."
(Uhhhhh laughs and looks around the room as if he has won a big victory. Then he notices no one else is laughing.)

Dr. S.A.Tea: Uhhhhh, try very, very hard to understand this. Although overall we are preparing for the SAT, right now we are discussing the essay, which is a short piece of writing.

Uhhhhh (going into sports mode): Gimme da ball, coach.

On the other hand . . .

An essay with a score of 1 (the lowest score):

An essay in this category is *fundamentally lacking*, demonstrating *very little* or *no mastery*, and is severely flawed by ONE OR MORE of the following weaknesses:

> - **Develops no viable point of view on the topic, or provides little or no evidence to support its position**
>
> - **Is disorganized or unfocused, resulting in a disjointed or incoherent essay**
>
> - **Displays fundamental errors in vocabulary**
>
> - **Demonstrates severe flaws in sentence structure**
>
> - **Contains pervasive errors in grammar, usage, or mechanics that persistently interfere with meaning**

What Does All that Mean?

Good development and organization are crucial for a good score on the essay.

1. Your paper should first state a clear point of view, and then go on to support that point of view in a structured and focused manner. If you examine the descriptions of the score of "6" and the score of "1" essays more closely, you will notice how the wording stands nearly at two opposite ends of the spectrum. A "6" essay "effectively and insightfully develops a point of view," while a "1" essay "develops no viable point of view." A "6" essay is "well organized and clearly focused," while a "1" essay is "disorganized or unfocused." Also, a "6" essay utilizes "clearly appropriate examples, reasons and other evidence to support its point of view," while a "1" essay "provides little or no evidence to support its position."

2. You will receive a higher score if your writing demonstrates good language skills and a strong vocabulary. Evaluating someone's writing is clearly a subjective process; still, it is clear that if you can use a variety of interesting words with great facility and if your writing is clear and smooth, that will gain you extra points.

How Much Time Do the Graders Spend on Each Essay and How Should that Impact How You Write an Essay?

Dr. S. A. Tea: What do you think the essay graders spend on each essay?

Wictoria: Twenty minutes?

Thor: Ten minutes?

Uhhhhh: Five dollars?

Dr. S. A. Tea: Uhhhhh! TIME! How much <u>time</u> do they spend? On the SAT II Writing Subject Test, the essay graders traditionally spend only a couple of minutes or so per essay. This is because the essays are being graded holistically.

Uhhhhh: So, uh, does that mean dat I get more points if I write about da Pope or someding?

Dr. S. A. Tea: Uhhhhh, holistically, not holy! In other words, the readers are looking at the overall effort. The readers understand that your paper is not going to be perfect and if you make a few errors, that is not going to seriously hinder your grade.

Thor: So, Doctor Du-hude, loike does that mean that we don't need to worry about going back to check our papers?

Dr. S. A. Tea: The key phrase was a "few errors." In your case, since you write like Gollum, it becomes very important to go back and fix as many mistakes as you can find. Let's talk about two of the most important components of the essay grading process: *Structure* and *Development*.

Dr. S. A. Tea's Tips for Structuring and Developing Your Essay:

1. Your essay is probably best structured in this format:

> - **Introduction**
>
> - **Two to four body paragraphs**
>
> - **A conclusion**

You can structure an essay any way you would like on the test, but keeping it simple is probably the best way to go.

2. The introduction should contain three thoughts: (1) what is the topic, (2) what is your opinion (thesis), and most importantly, (3) why you hold this opinion (one or two sentences that explain why you have formed that opinion). Too many students give an opinion but never get around to explaining why they hold this opinion in their introduction. For example, let's go back to the prompt we have already discussed: "Can one day make a difference in someone's life?" Here is an example of a weak introduction:

> *Spelling is my favorite thing in the world. The greatest day of my life was when I won the state spelling championship.*

Clearly this is not the most interesting introduction. Does anything about it make you want to read on? Now, if this student were to spruce up his writing with some more interesting phrases, the introduction becomes much stronger, as we see here:

To many, spelling is a dying art. With the advent of spellcheckers, many people wonder why they should bother learning to spell properly. I look at things differently. The greatest day of my life was when I won the state spelling championship. That day, all the hours I had spent searching countless dictionaries and drilling on endless lists of words finally led to a rewarding victory.

Pay attention, Du-hude!

3. The body paragraphs should back up your thesis with evidence. You should always try to use specific examples. For example, the student who wrote about winning the spelling championship should first perhaps describe the work he did leading up to the championship. Then perhaps he should describe the actual championship and the emotions that he felt before, during, and after the event.

4. The conclusion should summarize the paper and, if possible, introduce one new thought that ties into the thesis. For example, the student who wrote about the spelling championship could say:

My victory in the spelling state championship was very rewarding. However, in addition, I think that I have learned a lesson that has future ramifications. Proper spelling requires great discipline. The discipline that I learned from practicing for the spelling state championship has now become a permanent part of my character and will surely affect all of my future endeavors.

Don't write one long paragraph: Break up your essay.

5. Don't just write one long paragraph. Make it easy for the grader to read your paper. Break your essay up into different paragraphs.

6. As a general rule, don't put a lot of specific examples into the introduction. This tends to give the impression that you are already deviating from your thesis and you will likely be marked down for poor development. Let's say that a student is writing about her love of dance. Here is how a misplaced specific example could ruin an introduction:

> *Acting is the most wonderful thing in the world. The time I spend with my drama group is my favorite part of the day. One of my favorite actors in the world is Gilbert Gottfried. Sure, his voice is like mace to your ears, but who can forget the voice of the duck screeching "AFLAC! . . . AFLAC!"*

Obviously this kind of specific detail does not belong in your introduction.

What's the STA?

How Should You Choose a Direction in Your Essay?

Dr. S. A. Tea: As we could see from your first essays, obviously the direction you choose is very important. If you write about witches, or surfing, or shopping, or winning the league championship . . .

Uhhhhh, *waking up:* Let me at dose suckers, coach!

Dr. S. A. Tea, *continuing:* Anyway, if you write about these things, you've got to make them sound important. You've got to strive for <u>depth</u>.

Thor: You mean like a mondo fifty foot swell?

Xasmine: You mean, huh, like having a widely varied wardrobe?

Uhhhhh: You mean like when you die?

Dr. S. A. Tea: No, Uhhhhh! That's death! What I am talking about is actually writing about something important.

Dr. S. A. Tea's Tips for Picking a Good Topic for Your Essay

1. Stick to answering the question. If you are asked whom you would pick for a role model, it would not be good to write an essay about "My friend the carrot."

2. Pick one side or the other. There are no right answers. Let's say the question was, "Do you believe there should be a draft for the military?" If you feel that you can see both sides of the argument you should probably still pick one way or the other. If you try to cover too much ground, you may run out of time.

3. Write about something that falls within the range of normality. For example, don't write about the time you spent on the planet Septicor.

4. Try to pick an interesting topic and direction. If the question is, "Can one day make a difference in someone's life?" try to pick something that will really catch the reader's attention.

Practice Exercises

Okay, now it's your turn to be the judge. What follows are three introductions that address a topic. After each introduction there will be a space for you to write some comments. Do your best to evaluate the clarity of point of view, phrasing, and vocabulary. Then, in the appropriate space, rate the essays from best to worst.

Topic: Is disagreement always negative?

Intro #1

Disagreement is sometimes good and sometimes bad. It all depends on the person. It could be bad if you and the other end up fighting. It could be good if you express a viewpoint that is very important to you.

_____

_____

Intro #2

The word "disagreement" has a negative tone. After all, a disagreement sounds like a fight, and fights seem inherently evil. But is disagreement always negative? Sometimes a different point of view can spur new ideas and direction. Imagine if the colonists in the New World had not disagreed with the British monarchy? What if Galileo had gone along with the generally accepted view of the universe? In fact, much of history has been determined by disagreement. Disagreement has not only affected politics, but history, science, and the arts.

_____

_____

Intro #3

Disagreement is always bad. When my mom and me argue, we get into some wicket fights. Once I tore her wig off. Boy, am I suprised. She is bald!

_____

_____

Rate the introductions from best to worst:

Intro #1 _____

Intro #2 _____

Intro #3 _____

Dr. S. A. Tea's Comments on the Introductions

Intro # 1

Bland. No words catch your eye. No interesting thoughts. Awkward phrasing like *you and the other end up fighting.*

Intro #2

Strong. Immediately establishes the writer's point of view that disagreement is often positive and necessary for society to progress. Interesting phrasing and great vocabulary.

Intro #3

Weak. Awkward language like *When my mom and me argue,* etc. . . . Writing-tense problems and misspellings like *Boy, am I suprised* and *wicket.* In addition, the way in which the specific example is used gives the introduction the feel of a diary.

Ranking:

Intro #1 ___2___

Intro #2 ___1___

Intro #3 ___3___

2-21-2, What Does that Mean?

Dr. S. A. Tea: Class, let me throw some numbers at you: 2-21-2 . . . Does anyone have any idea what these numbers might mean?

Uhhhhh, *all excited:* Yeah . . . dat's my play number. When the quarterback calls that play I'm sposed to run da post pattern.

Wictoria: I think that's the combination of my locker at school.

Uboreme: Those are the measurements of my girlfriend.

Dr. S. A. Tea: What?

Uboreme: Yeah, I go for the thin look.

Dr. S. A. Tea: Come on, Uboreme, that can't be your girlfriend's measurements. What's the name of this girl?

Uboreme: Bulimia Permanente.

Zino: Ees that some sorta Cuban name? I knew a family named Permanente once.

Dr. S. A. Tea: It's a joke, Zino.

Zino: Oh, you wacky Americanos. I geet eet. Bulimia Permanente. That's idiot.

Dr. S. A. Tea: Zino, the phrase is "That's dope."

Zino: Dope, idiot . . . what's the difference.

Dr. S.A. Tea's Tips for Time Management (2-21-2)

1. Two minutes to think over your direction. Too many students jump into the essay without thinking it over first. Take a little time to make sure of the direction you would like to take. Because you don't have time to write a full outline, it might be smart to jot down a few quick ideas.

2. Twenty-one minutes to write your essay. Obviously the bulk of your time should be spent writing the actual essay.

3. Two minutes to read over the essay and correct errors. Most students never take a second look at their essays. Be smart: Go back to check for grammatical errors, spelling errors, awkward sentences, etc.

2-21-2: Think about it, write it, go back and check yourself over.

Presenting Yourself as an Intelligent Person in the Essay

Dr. S. A. Tea: Now, although we have a lot of very bright people in this class, some of you come across poorly in your essays.

Uhhhhh, *to himself:* Ball, hoop. Ball, hoop.

Dr. S. A. Tea: And then some of you come across poorly in everything . . .

Tip

Dr. S. A. Tea's Tips for How to Make Yourself Sound More Intelligent in Your Essay

1. Make yourself sound literate by using good examples. Obviously, the more literate you sound, the better off you are. The directions for the essay specifically state, "Support your view with an example or examples from literature, the arts, history, politics, science and technology, current events, or your experience or observation." The College Board Web site lists an example of an essay that two readers gave a "6" (the highest score). The essay writer uses *King Lear,* the Shakespeare play, as the main example in this paper. Obviously if you are quoting from Shakespeare or using an example from Dickens, or referring to any other literary reference, this clearly gives a reader the impression that you are intelligent. Historical examples are also great references. The College Board Web site also lists an essay that received a "5" (the second-highest score) from two readers. This essay refers to Martin Luther King, Jr. You could also pick examples from movies, personal experiences, etc. It is extremely important to have at least one or two examples in your essay. If you just express opinions in your essay and never back them up with examples, your essay will lack depth.

2. Stay away from slang and *Webbish*. It is crucial to separate your normal, everyday conversation from a formal English essay. For example, if you are trying to say something was marvelous, don't use the slang phrase "It was the world." Also, many of you are using the Internet constantly. The Internet has helped create a whole new language, *Webbish*. In a sense, a good portion of *Webbish* is sort of a modernized shorthand. If you use email and spend time in Internet chat rooms, you may have become accustomed to using abbreviations like "b/c" for "because" and "&" for "and." Slang and abbreviations are likely to have a negative effect on your essay grade. It's much better to use formal English. Get it? :)

3. Make sure that your essay is not too short. The "6" essay that is provided as an example on the College Board Web site is more than 350 words long. The "5" and "4" essays that are shown as examples on the College Board Web site are barely above 250 words. I have graded essays that were only 100 words long and the sheer shortness of these essays gave a bad impression right off the bat.

Make it Easy on Your Grader: Handwriting and Spelling

Dr. S. A. Tea: Now we come to another issue, handwriting*. Technically the essay graders are not supposed to mark you down for poor handwriting, but let's be realistic . . .

Here's a sample of Xasmine's writing:

My mom was all let's go and get our nails done.

Here's a sample of Wictoria's writing:

It takes a good deal of discipline to learn how to wave your wand properly.

---

* Computers will be made available only to candidates with a disability that requires use of a computer.

Conversation with Wictoria about her cat

Dr. S.A.Tea: So, Wictoria, tell me about your cat.

Wictoria: I hate this cat! I'm allergic to it and it's always climbing all over my face.

Dr. S.A.Tea: So, why do you have the cat?

Wictoria: I'm a witch in training and I thought I'd improve my image by getting a black cat. I don't know why it won't behave.

Dr. S.A.Tea: Maybe you crossed its path.

Wictoria: Very funny.

Dr. S. A. Tea: Wictoria, clearly you are a good writer. Based on the content of these two sentences, you would be heading for a better grade than Xasmine. However, your handwriting is atrocious. I know that you have written "Wave your wand," but to a normal person this almost looks like "Wae your wad." You sound like Elmer Fudd! Put yourselves in the position of the essay graders. If they have only a few minutes to read your essay, how happy are they going to be about trying to decipher something completely illegible? As fair as the graders try to be, bad handwriting certainly is not going to help your grade.

(Scene switches to a university in the year 2204.)

Grad Student: Professor, we've just deciphered that writing from the early 21st century!

Professor: Great, great! Was it a passionate statement protesting the possibility of nuclear war? Was it a paper that highlighted the plight of the starving?

Grad Student: No, no. It was that weird Wictoria writing her wacky witch stuff again.

(Back to the class)

Dr. S. A. Tea: Now we come to the arena of spelling and misuse of words. Let's take a quick look at a sentence from Uhhhhh's paper,

> *"Aftur we scored, the nose of the crowd was defecating."*

Dr. S. A. Tea: Uhhhhh, first of all, let's look at what it appears you are saying. Ignoring the pitiful spelling of "after," you are stating that the crowd's nose is emptying its bowels. I think what you mean to say is: "After we scored, the noise of the crowd was deafening."

Uhhhhh: Yeah. Dat's it. I heard John Madden say dat once.

Dr. S. A. Tea's Tips for Handwriting and Spelling

1. Pretend that you are a grader reading your essay. Is it legible? Take an extra few seconds to clean up areas that are not legible.

2. If you know that your cursive writing is not legible, consider printing your essay. It may take you longer to print your essay, but if this means that the graders will actually be able to read what you wrote, it's well worth it.

3. If you are writing a live essay and you don't know how to spell a word, pick another word. The essay graders have absolutely no idea what word you are going to use.

4. When you are at home, work on your spelling by using the spellchecker as a learning tool, not just a corrective device. If you are weak at spelling, you know part of the problem is that you have learned to rely too heavily on the spellchecker. In fact, sometimes you may be relying so heavily on the spellchecker that you may end up picking the wrong word altogether. When you are at home, use the spellchecker to help you identify which parts of the sentences are *possibly* incorrect. Then look at the underlined words and make a guess on your own as to a possible correction. After that, look at the spellchecker's suggestion. If you continue to rely just on the spellchecker's suggestions, you will never improve your spelling.

If you don't know how to spell a word, pick another word.

Dr. S. A. Tea: Although there are many grammatical errors that irritate me, there's one particular error that bothers me more than all the rest.

Class, *in unison:* What is it, Dr. S. A. Tea? We're your friend's; if there are thing's that bother you, you can tell us.

Dr. S. A. Tea: Arggggggggggh!

Dr. S. A. Tea's No. 1 Pet Peeve

1. Beware of the "Super Apostrophe." Let's face it; everywhere you turn you see extra apostrophes. It's almost as if everyone thinks that adding extra apostrophes is a great way to make a phrase even better. A magazine's front page headline reads, "Winter Is On It's Way." One of the country's biggest newspapers runs a story on the "SAT's." These are clearly misuses of an apostrophe. What is the proper use of an apostrophe? There are several instances in which it is considered acceptable to use an apostrophe. Apostrophes primarily suggest possession. For example, the following phrase uses an apostrophe properly, "This is Joe's baseball." A contraction is an example of the proper use of an apostrophe. *It's* is a contraction of the phrase "it is." In addition, there are instances when using an apostrophe clarifies what you are saying. For example, if you are writing a math problem and you want to express the plural of *X*, it is probably clearer to use *X's* than *Xs*. But let's draw the line somewhere. You've all seen the signs outside a family's house that tells you the family name. If your family name is Cook and you put up a sign outside your house saying, "We're the Cook's," you better hope he's not a cannibal. (If you don't get that joke, have someone explain it to you.) Use apostrophes responsibly and stay away from the "Super Apostrophe."

Practice Exercises

Now let's give you a chance to evaluate an essay. What follows is a very poorly written essay. First, read the essay and circle as many errors as you can find. When you are finished finding mistakes in the essay, answer the multiple-choice questions that follow.

Horrible Essay

Prompt: *Who controls your happiness: you, or the outside world?*

Happiness is a wonderful thing, we should all try to attain it. I believe that I control my own happiness. The happiest day of my life was when I got my kitten, Sandy. You should have seen the look on her face when she new that she is going to be leaving the pet shop and that she is going to be our's.

Over the years, Sandy has recieved a bunch of attention from her owners. Us. Once she did the silliest thing that effected everyone in the family. Sandy tried to catch a spider that was crawling outside the window on the third floor! Luckily when Sandy jumped she hit the screen but she hit it so hard that she knocked it partially out & she was dangling from the windowsill.

We were all out side. My brother was getting ready for the big game. His team won that day. When I saw Sandy, I was paralleled with fear. But I took a deep breath, ran inside, and grabbed Sandy just in the nick of time. Go me! Maybe at this point I should say why we named our cat, Sandy. My father and I came up with the name when we picked her up at the pet store. At the same time we both decide to say, "Let's call her Sandy." The funny thing is that I wanted to call her Sandy because she was the color of sand & my father wanted to call her Sandy because she looked like some old baseball player named Sandy Cofax or something. My dad is so weird! Anyway, Sandy it was.

In conclusion, clearly one controls one's own happiness. It doesn't have to be a cat that makes you happy. Every person is in charge of their own happiness.

Essay Analysis

Wooscious!

1. Does the essay have a proper structure: introduction, body paragraphs, and a conclusion?

A) Yes, it should win a Pulitzer Prize for writing.

B) Yes, this is the koolest essay I have ever red! I have a kat named Sandy to.

C) No. By the way, what is an essay?

D) Yes, the essay has a proper structure. The problem is what is contained within the structure: the abominable writing.

2. Is the introduction strong? If not, what makes it weak?

A) Yes. It is strong like a bull.

B) No. It didn't eat its Wheaties.

C) Yes. If I could write like this I wouldn't be spending my fourth year in a row as a junior.

D) No. First of all, the introduction is bland. An essay grader will most likely lose interest immediately because the writer has nothing interesting to say and no interesting way to say it. Also, although the writer states that she believes she controls her own happiness, she never states *why* in the introduction. Finally, the writer makes the mistake of putting a specific example (when she got her kitten from the pet shop) in the introduction.

3. Is the conclusion strong? If not, what makes it weak?

A) Yes. It made me laugh, it made me cry. (Oh wait, that was the movie *Titanic*.)

B) Yes. It is strong like other bull.

C) No. Once again the writer says nothing interesting. In addition, she has been writing in first voice and all of a sudden she uses the word *one*. Finally, she uses a singular noun, *person,* in one sentence and then the plural *their* in the next sentence to refer to the same person.

D) No. The essay isn't strong, but I am strong. Did you know that I can bench-press two hundred pounds with my left pinkie?

4. Does the writer do a good job of using specific examples to show how her cat made her happy?

A) No. I have tried to find a cat that would make me happy for years, but every time I pick one out it surrounds my throat and tries to strangle me. Oh, wait, I'm getting cats mixed up with Anacondas.

B) No. The writer starts to mention an incident with Sandy, but then never shows how this incident relates to her happiness. She also describes how Sandy was named, but again the writer never shows how this contributed to her happiness.

C) Yes. It made me laugh, it made me cry. (Oh, wait, sorry . . . I'm thinking of *Titanic* again.)

D) Yes. Stop already with the "it made me laugh, it made me cry."

5. Does the writer stick to one voice throughout the essay?

A) No. At the beginning she sounds more like Barry White, but by the end she's hitting those high notes like Mariah Carey.

B) No. When you are writing, there are no voices. There's only the sound of pencil on paper.

C) No. Just in paragraph 1 alone the author uses three pronouns: *we, I* and *you*. She probably would have been fine if she had just used *we* and *I*, but switching to addressing the reader in the "you" form immediately gives the essay a disorganized feel. In the conclusion, the writer moves to using *one,* which furthers the confusion.

D) Yes. I hear voices in my head all the time.

6. Does the essay wander?

A) Yes. No. What was the question again?

B) No. Don't be silly: Essays can't move.

C) Yes. In paragraph 2 the writer is describing an incident with Sandy. However, instead of relating that to the topic, "happiness," the writer makes an abrupt shift in paragraph 3 and talks about her brother. Then later in the same paragraph the writer relates an inappropriate story about how Sandy was named. The essay truly never has any direction.

D) No. But boy, the guy who wrote answer (C) sure is anal. Can't he just say yes or no like the rest of us?

Answer key:
1) D   2) D   3) C   4) B   5) C   6) C

Okay, now here is the essay with all of the errors circled.

Marked Errors for Essay

Happiness is a wonderful thing, we should all try to attain it. I believe that I control my own happiness. The happiest day of my life was when I got my kitten, Sandy. You should have seen the look on her face when she (new) that she (is) going to be leaving the pet shop and that she (is) going to be (our's)

Over the years, Sandy has (recieved) a bunch of attention from her owners. (Us) Once she did the silliest thing that (effected) everyone in the family. Sandy tried to catch a spider that was crawling outside the window on the third floor! Luckily when Sandy jumped she hit the screen but she hit it so hard that she knocked it partially out (&) she was dangling from the windowsill.

We were all out side. My brother was getting ready for the big game. His team won that day. When I saw Sandy, I was paralleled with fear. But I took a deep breath, ran inside, and grabbed Sandy just in the nick of time. Go me! Maybe at this point I should say why we named our cat, Sandy. My father and I came up with the name when we picked her up at the pet store. At the same time we both decide to say, "Let's call her Sandy." The funny thing is that I wanted to call her Sandy because she was the color of sand & my father wanted to call her Sandy because she looked like some old baseball player named Sandy Cofax or something. My dad is so weird! Anyway, Sandy it was.

In conclusion, clearly one controls one's own happiness. It doesn't have to be a cat that makes you happy. Every person is in charge of their own happiness.

Dr. S. A. Tea's Essay Analysis

As you can see from what is marked above, there are at least 16 basic errors in this essay.

Spelling Errors:

There are actually five spelling errors. In paragraph 1, *knew* is misspelled. In paragraph 2, the words *received* and *affected* are misspelled. Finally, in paragraph 3, the words *outside* and *Koufax* are misspelled.

Punctuation Errors:

There are several punctuation errors. In paragraph 1, there should be a semi-colon, not a comma, before the word *we*. In addition, there is no need for the apostrophe in the word *ours*. In paragraph 2, there should be a comma, not a period before the word *us*. Obviously, also the *u* in *us* should not be capitalized. The last sentence of paragraph 2 should be broken up into two sentences.

Diction Errors (Misuse of Words):

In the fourth sentence of paragraph 3, the writer uses the phrase, "paralleled with fear." This should obviously be "paralyzed with fear."

Abbreviation/Slang Errors:

In the third to last sentence of paragraph 3, the writer uses an ampersand instead of writing *and*. Also, in the middle of paragraph 3, the writer uses the phrase, "Go me!" which is obviously too informal.

Verb Tense Errors:

In the last sentence of paragraph 1, the writer begins in the past tense and then switches to the present tense for the remainder of the sentence. It would have been better to word the entire sentence in the past tense. Similarly in paragraph 3 towards the end of the paragraph, the writer says, "At the same time we both decide to say . . ." Instead of *decide* the writer should have used the word *decided* to keep the sentence completely in the past tense.

Why does Wictoria keep asking me to check out the bottom of her cauldron?

What's Your Score?

Okay, now let's total it up. Give yourself one point for each error you found in the essay and each multiple-choice question you got right.

Examining an Excellent Essay

Now that you have examined a poor essay, let's look at an excellent one.

There are some who say that one day can change the entire direction of your life. The day that changed my life was when I won the Young American Pianist and Violinist Contest. Finishing first was an epiphany; I had never won anything before and the enthusiasm I gained from this first victory bolstered my desire to become a professional musician.

I can still remember when I first started taking piano lessons at the age of eight. Even though my fingers made mistakes, there was magic when I struck the perfect chord or played a clean arpeggio. My piano teacher introduced me to the music of Beethoven and Mozart and I felt an instant sense of familarity. The chords and melodies that these composers used were very similar to the music I had always heard in my head before I fell asleep each night.

For nine years, I practiced piano four hours each day. To be frank, though, when I turned seventeen I started to burn out. When I would practice, my hands would feel wooden and I couldn't concentrate. In retrospect, perhaps I no longer had any motivation or goals. I was truly at the point of quitting.

One day, I received a call from my piano teacher. She told me about the Young American Pianist Music Contest and suggested that I enter the competition. I decided to give music one last shot. When I took the stage the night of the contest, a powerful feeling came over me. I played my first notes and I was filled with a sense of confidence. I performed Mendelssohn's *Spinning Song* perfectly. When I found out that I had won the contest, I finally felt as if all the efforts in the previous years I had spent and everything I had worked on were worthwhile.

Music is a strange mistress. Just at the time in my life when I was sure I wanted nothing more to do with her, she rewarded me. Winning the music competition had a permanent effect on me. Now that I have confidence in my ability to perform, I am considering making music my career.

Conversation with Uhhhhh about cheating

Dr. S.A.Tea: Uhhhhh, I've read your most recent essay and I know you copied someone else's paper.

Uhhhhh: How d'ya know dat?

Dr. S.A.Tea: Well, for one thing the writing actually made sense, but I think what really gave it away was when you started the essay by saying, "My name is Uboreme."

Quick Evaluation of the Essay:

This is an excellent essay. The first thing to notice is the strong structure and development in the essay. In addition, the author clearly demonstrates a great sense of vocabulary and phrasing. The essay is not perfect; there is at least one spelling error, "familiarity," and one run-on sentence, "When I found out that I had won the contest, I finally felt as if all the efforts in the previous years I had spent and everything I had worked on were worthwhile." Nonetheless, this is an example of an essay that might earn a "6" with the essay graders.

Practice Exercises

Now it's your turn. Here are three different topics. Set a timer for 25 minutes and then write an essay on one topic. Remember the tips we have discussed. After you have finished writing, make a photocopy of your essay. First, do a self-evaluation of your work. Then give the photocopy of the essay to a good reader. When the reader has finished evaluating your essay, examine his (her) comments to see what other improvements you can make.

Over a period of days, try to write essays on all three topics. You will make the greatest improvements if you:

1. Follow the tips in this chapter

2. Do a good job of self-correcting the essays

3. Have someone who is a great reader evaluate your essays

Topic 1: Is anger generally a positive or negative force in people's lives?

Topic 2: Do we control our own destinies or is much of our destiny dictated for us?

Topic 3: Is war sometimes necessary?

Grammar Section

Dr. S. A. Tea: Now we're going to move on to the grammar section . . .

Xasmine: Kelsey Grammer? Oh, he's so cool! I so love *Frasier.* Do you remember the show when Daphne and Niles . . .

Dr. S. A. Tea, *cutting her off:* No, actually Xasmine, we're going to work on the grammar section — how to write proper English. You know, the language you don't speak . . .

Xasmine: "The language you don't speak . . ." You mean sign language?

My mom was all let's go and get our nails done.

Dr. S. A. Tea: Never mind. There are three types of questions in the grammar area of the New SAT. First we have *Identifying Sentence Errors.* In this section, you merely determine which part of a sentence is incorrect. The second section is *Improving Sentences.* In this section, you actually fix the sentences. The final section is *Improving Paragraphs.* In this section, you are given questions based on a short reading passage. Here you essentially are trying to improve paragraphs by fixing sentences and moving sentences around in the passage.

The crucial thing is that all three of these grammar sections overlap each other. Although technically there are three different sections, the types of errors you are searching for are often the same from section to section.

Dr. S. A. Tea's Tips for Avoiding Errors in the Multiple-Choice Grammar Sections:

There are four main types of errors to look for on all three of the multiple-choice grammar sections: (1) "matching," (2) "vagueness," (3) "hillbilly English," and (4) "awkwardness."

Before we look at the actual question types, let's examine some common errors you will be looking for throughout the entire grammar section.

1. Matching

Dr. S. A. Tea: When it comes to grammar, how many of you understand what I mean by using the word "matching"?

Xasmine, *waving her hand:* El Doctor, El Doctor! I tried a matching service on the Web once, but they hooked me up with some geek who kept spamming me . . .

Make sure that nouns and verbs "match up."

Dr. S. A. Tea: No, Xasmine, not that kind of matching. What I mean by matching is making sure that everything lines up within the question (verbs, nouns, tenses, etc.).

Practice Exercises

Here are a few examples of "matching" errors. See if you can rewrite these sentences to fix the grammar problems.

1. When I was young, my parents were very careful about making you follow their guidelines.

_____

_____

2. Billy will probably get the job because his work ethic, cheerfulness, and accountability is just what employers are looking for.

_____

_____

3. The gardener thinks that Mrs. Smith has asked him to water the plants yesterday.

_____

_____

4. The pizza that we ordered to be sent to the house was much worse than Gino's Pizza restaurant.

_____

_____

5. Jim was whistling, dancing, and had a smile on his face.

_____

_____

Now compare your answers to the corrections below:

Maintaining the same voice:

*1. When I was young, my parents were very careful about making **me** follow their guidelines.*

In the incorrect sentence, the voices don't match: The writer goes from *I* to *you*. The new sentence fixes this problem by replacing *you* with *me*.

Noun/Verb agreement:

*2. Billy will probably get the job because his work ethic, cheerfulness, and accountability **are** just what employers are looking for.*

In the incorrect sentence, the problem is the word *is*. Since there are three nouns: *work ethic, cheerfulness,* and *accountability, is* should be changed to *are*.

Verb agreement:

*3. The gardener thinks that Mrs. Smith **asked** him to water the plants yesterday.*

In the incorrect sentence, the words *has asked* don't match up with the word *yesterday*. The new sentence fixes that problem by replacing *has asked* with *asked*.

Improper Comparisons:

*4. The pizza that we ordered to be sent to the house was much worse **than the pizza** from Gino's pizza restaurant.*

Here you once again need to fight against what is considered fine in normal conversation. The problem with the incorrect sentence is that it makes a comparison between a pizza and a restaurant. The new sentence fixes that problem by changing the end of the sentence to "the pizza from Gino's pizza restaurant."

Parallel Structure:

*5. Jim was whistl**ing**, danc**ing**, and smil**ing**.*

If you look at the original sentence, "Jim was whistling, dancing, and had a smile on his face," you will notice that the last part of the sentence, "had a smile on his face," is not parallel with whistling and dancing. By rewriting this sentence and using *smiling,* you have established a parallel structure, "whistl**ing**, danc**ing**, and smil**ing**." This also helps to shorten the sentence.

2. Vagueness

Dr. S. A. Tea: Next, let's move on to another type of error to look for—vagueness. Who understands what I am talking about?

Zino: Monsieur Docteur, I am not zo shure whut yeuh mean by vagueness, could yeuh be more specifique?

Dr. S. A. Tea: Very funny, Zino...Here are some examples of vagueness.

Practice Exercises

Here are two examples of vague sentences. See if you can rewrite these sentences to fix the grammar problems.

1. The manager told her assistant that she had to work late.

_____

_____

2. Because she wrote novels at an amazing rate, prolific is the best way to describe Agatha Christie.

_____

_____

Now compare your answers to the corrections below:

Noun reference:

The manager told the assistant to work late.

The problem with the incorrect sentence is that it is not clear who has to work late, the manager or the assistant. The new sentence clarifies that it is the assistant who needs to work late.

Specifying the noun immediately after a clause:

Because she wrote novels at an amazing pace, Agatha Christie can best be described as prolific.

In the incorrect sentence, the first part, "Because she wrote novels at a prolific pace," never specifies who writes the novels. Therefore, immediately after the first comma, the novelist, Agatha Christie, should be named.

3. Hillbilly English

Uhhhhh: Dis stuff being so hard. I don't understand none of it.

Dr. S. A. Tea: Thank you, Uhhhhh. What a great introduction to the next topic that we need to discuss: *Hillbilly English*.

Practice Exercises

No Hillbillies here!

Here are two examples of sentences that feature *Hillbilly English*. See if you can rewrite these sentences to fix the problem.

1. There are hardly no days when it doesn't rain.

_____

_____

2. Magellan was the first person to circumvent the world.

_____

_____

Now compare your answers to the corrections below:

Double Negatives:

There are hardly **any** days when it doesn't rain.

In the hills, the incorrect sentence might win a Pulitzer Prize. (Hey, it's got a couple of words with two syllables!) But here in the world of formal English, you have to change the word *no* to *any*.

Misuse of Words:

Magellan was the first person to **circumnavigate** the world.

Unless Magellan was the first astronaut, the first sentence is incorrect. *Circumvent* means "to avoid." The incorrect sentence can be fixed by substituting *circumnavigate* for *circumvent.*

4. Awkwardness

Dr. S. A. Tea: Obviously for most of the grammar section you are searching for basic grammatical errors. However, the test makers also want to see if you can recognize and fix cumbersome sentences or phrasing. (This is especially true on the *Improving Sentences* and *Improving Paragraphs* sections.) In other words, you want to pick answers that make the sentences less awkward.

Xasmine: Les who?

Dr. S. A. Tea: Less awkward.

Xasmine: Never heard of him.

Dr. S. A. Tea: Never mind, Xasmine. It's when you *do* understand that I will be worried.

Practice Exercises

1. If you have a choice between the two sentences below, why is the second one better?

Daniel composed symphonies and they resonated with complicated jazz voicings.

Daniel composed symphonies that resonated with complicated jazz voicings.

Although both sentences are grammatically correct, in the second example you have made the same point more <u>concisely</u> (in a shorter sentence).

2. If you have a choice between the two sentences below, why is the second one better?

Jane was known for writing books of short stories that centered on the lives of animals; in all of her books these themes were included.

Jane was known for writing books of short stories that centered on the lives of animals; she always included these themes in her work.

Although both sentences are grammatically correct, in the second example you have used the active voice. This is because the author is *including* the themes as opposed to having them *included* in her work.

Now let's move on to the actual multiple-choice question types on the grammar portion of the New SAT.

Identifying Sentence Errors

Dr. S. A. Tea: Let's talk about *Identifying Sentence Errors*.

Uboreme, *finally becoming excited*: SAT man, good move! This is actually a critical issue that I would like to discuss. Do you know that there are thousands of prisoners across the world who have received unfair sentences and shouldn't be in jail at all?

Dr. S. A. Tea: Uboreme, that's fascinating, except that we are talking about the grammar section on the SAT called *Identifying Sentence Errors*.

Uboreme: Oh . . .

First, let's look at the question type, *Identifying Sentence Errors.* Here are the directions for this section as they have appeared on the College Board Web site.

Directions: The following sentences test your knowledge of grammar, usage, diction (choice of words), and idioms. Some sentences are correct. No sentence contains more than one error. You will find that the error, if there is one, is underlined and lettered. Elements of the sentence that are not underlined will not be changed. In choosing answers, follow the requirements of standard written English. If there is an error, select the <u>one underlined part</u> that must be changed to make the sentence correct and fill in the corresponding oval on the answer sheet.

If there is no error, fill in answer oval (E).

EXAMPLE:	SAMPLE ANSWER

The red chipmunks <u>approached</u> a   A B Ⓒ D E
                    A

<u>large</u> group of birds that backed
   B

off from <u>it</u> <u>rapidly</u>. <u>No error.</u>
        C   D   E

Dr. S. A. Tea's Tips For "Identifying Sentence Errors"

1. Remember to look for the four types of errors we have discussed: matching, vagueness, hillbilly English, and awkwardness. Try to look for mistakes that violate the rules of "formal" English.

2. Whatever is not underlined is correct. Use what is not underlined to help make proper decisions about verb tenses, noun usage, etc.

3. On average, one out of five times there is no error.

Practice Exercises

Here are five Identifying Sentence Errors questions. The answers and explanations can be found after the questions.

1. My friend, <u>being</u> my <u>best</u> friend in the world, <u>has asked</u> me if I
         A   B   C

would like to travel with him to Europe <u>this</u> summer. <u>No error</u>.
                                     D   E

2. On the radio <u>they</u> said that the vote <u>would be</u> very close and
             A   B

that it wouldn't be clear <u>until</u> morning <u>which</u> candidate had won
                       C   D

the election. <u>No error</u>.
            E

3. The distance <u>between</u> the two friends grew <u>ever</u> greater as
              A   B

<u>they</u> spoke <u>less</u> frequently. <u>No error</u>.
 C   D   E

4. The <u>use</u> of the Internet in schools permits students to gather data
     A

from different parts <u>of</u> the world and, more importantly, <u>free</u> them from
             B   C

the slower process of searching <u>through</u> library books. <u>No error</u>.
                            D   E

5. <u>Because</u> of the <u>stimulating</u> conversation that was taking place
    A   B

in the room, Darlene <u>did</u> not feel the <u>affect</u> of the music. <u>No error</u>.
                     C   D   E

Answer Key:
1) A   2) A   3) E   4) C   5) D

Conversation with Zino about what "no error" means

Dr. S.A.Tea: Zino, I noticed that on every one of the Identifying Sentence Errors questions, you picked (E) No Error. Did you really feel that there was nothing wrong with any of the sentences?

Zino: On ze contrary, Herr Doctor. I always pick "E" because it iss grammatically incorrect.

Dr. S.A.Tea: What are you talking about?

Zino: "No Error" iss not a complete sentence.

Dr. S.A.Tea: Zino! While that is true, that is not the sentence we are evaluating. Think of an answer as an abbreviation for "There is not an error in the sentence."

Zino: No vunder I got every vun of zose questions wrong. The test people should be clearer with zuch matters.

EXPLANATIONS:

1) (A) is the best answer because the use of the word "being" is essentially a good example of *Hillbilly English*. "Who is" would have been more appropriate.

2) (A) is the best answer because "they" is too vague. "They" does not refer back to any specific noun.

3) (E) is the best answer because there is no error in this sentence.

4) (C) is the best answer because "free" is incorrect. It should be "frees" to match up properly with "The use of the Internet."

5) (D) is the best answer because the word should be "effect" and not "affect."

Improving Sentences

Dr. S. A. Tea: Let's talk about the next grammar section, *Improving Sentences*.

Uboreme: SAT man, this is also a crucial issue! Do you know what's it like to serve a sentence in a jail these days? The conditions are appalling!

Dr. S. A. Tea: Uboreme, I am glad that you empathize with all of these prisoners, however, now we are talking about the grammar section on the SAT called *Improving Sentences.*

Uboreme: Oh . . .

Now let's look at the question type, *Improving Sentences.* Here are the directions for this section as they have appeared on the College Board web site.

Directions: The following sentences test correctness and effectiveness of expressions. In choosing answers, follow the requirements of standard written English; that is, pay attention to grammar, choice of words, sentence corrections, and punctuation. In each of the following sentences, part of the sentence or the entire sentence is underlined. Beneath each sentence you will find five ways of phrasing the underlined part. Choice (A) repeats the original; the other four are different. Choose the answer that best expresses the meaning of the original sentence. If you think the original is better than any of the alternatives, choose it; otherwise choose one of the others. Your choice should produce the most effective sentence-clear and precise, without awkwardness or ambiguity.

EXAMPLE:	SAMPLE ANSWER

I have three favorite sports: running, swimming, <u>and when I bicycle</u>.

A Ⓑ C D E

A) and when I bicycle

B) and bicycling

C) and when I use the bicycle

D) and getting on the bicycle

E) and the times when I bicycle

Dr. S. A. Tea's Tips for "Improving Sentences"

"Less awkward" means smoother and more concise.

1. On *Improving Sentences* questions, answer (A) repeats the original sentence. Answer (A) is the answer you should pick when you feel that there is no error with the original sentence. Remember this is different than the previous section, *Identifying Sentence Errors*, where answer (E) was the answer to pick when you felt there was no error in the sentence.

2. Whatever is not underlined in the original sentence is correct. Use what is not underlined in the original sentence to help make proper decisions about verb tense, noun usage, etc.

3. Remember to look for the four types of errors we have discussed: matching, vagueness, hillbilly English, and

awkwardness. Try to look for mistakes that violate the rules of "formal" English.

4. Try to notice the "little" differences between the answers. Often two answers will be almost identical.

Example:

Billy and Jamie are the two best players on the team.
               <u>or</u>
Billy and Jamie is the best players on the team.

In a case like this, if you can notice the distinction between *are* and *is* you will probably pick the right answer.

5. On average, one out of five times there is no error.

A "Very" interesting conversation with Thor about college

Dr. S.A.Tea: Thor, would you like to go to college?

Thor: Very.

Dr. S.A.Tea: What?

Thor: Doctor Du-hude you asked me if I wanted to go to college and I said "Very."

Dr. S.A.Tea: But, Thor, that doesn't make any sense. You can't just say, "Very." You could say, "Very much" or "I would like to go to college very much," but you can't just say "Very." "Very" is an adverb; it modifies other words. If you use the word "very," you have to have a word following it.

Thor: Doctor Du-hude, but that's just dog. I don't need any extra words. I just want to say "Very."

Dr. S.A.Tea: You can't do that, Thor. No one is going to understand you. You have to have a word following "very."

Thor: Okay Du-hude, ask me again.

Dr. S.A.Tea: Okay, Thor would you like to go to college?

Thor: Yes, I very do.

Dr. S.A.Tea: Arrrrrrrrrrrrrrrgh!

Practice Exercises

Here are five *Improving Sentences* questions. The answers and explanations can be found after the questions.

1. While the music that he composed is difficult to categorize, <u>the legacy of George Gershwin remains clear</u>.

A) the legacy of George Gershwin remains clear

B) the legacy of George Gershwin was never clearer

C) George Gershwin's legacy is clear

D) George Gershwin left a legacy that remains clear

E) the leg of George Gershwin remains clear

2. The highway was <u>congested, filled with city dwellers streaming to the beach</u> for the weekend.

A) congested, filled with city dwellers streaming to the beach

B) congested; filled with city dwellers streaming to the beach

C) filled with city dwellers congested with the beach

D) congested and filled with city dwellers looking to stream to the beach

E) congested with beaches streaming with city dwellers

3. The soccer team was renowned for its punishing offense, <u>the way they played tenacious defense</u>, and refined behavior.

A) the way they played tenacious defense

B) the way they were played defense

C) tenacious defense

D) the way they defended so tenaciously

E) their defense that was tenacious

4. James Joyce was one of the first authors to write using the style now called "stream of consciousness"; for Joyce, thoughts, <u>rather than description and dialogue, were what was included as the main focus of his novels</u>.

A) rather than description and dialogue, were what was included as the main focus of his novels

B) rather than description and dialogue were included in his writing

C) rather than the inclusion of description and dialogue

D) rather than description and dialogues, were the main focus of his novels

E) rather than the novels were included as description and dialogue

5. Even though the girls' volleyball team should win the game, <u>there's no assurances that it will</u>.

A) there's no assurances that it will

B) there's no assurances that they will

C) there are no assurances that it will

D) there are no assurance that they will

E) there's no assurance that they will

Answer key:
1) D   2) A   3) C   4) D   5) C

EXPLANATIONS:

1) (D) is the best answer because the person, George Gershwin, must be named immediately after the comma.

2) (A) is the best answer because there is no error.

3) (C) is the best answer because "tenacious defense" creates a parallel structure with "punishing offense" and "refined behavior."

4) (D) is the best answer because it is the smoothest sentence and it uses a slightly more active voice.

5) (C) is the best answer. In every other answer there is some sort of grammatical error. The volleyball team is singular, so it must be referred to with an "it." Also, "assurances" is plural so you must say "there **are** no assurances."

What's Your Score?

Okay, now let's total your score from <u>both</u> the *Identifying Sentence Errors* exercise and the *Improving Sentences* exercise. Give yourself one point for each answer you got right.

If you scored

8-10 points	**When it comes to grammar, you're a bad gramma jamma!**
4-7 points	**When it comes grammar to, work you need some.**
0-3 points	**Why you keep talking about grandma? I love my grandma!**

Megacorrecting

Dr. S. A. Tea: Before we continue on to the *Improving Paragraphs* section, I want to discuss one other thing. Uboreme, I noticed that on the *Identifying Sentence Errors* section, you never picked (E) — no error — and on the *Improving Sentences* section, you never picked (A) — no error.

Uboreme: That's right. There's nothing in the world that is completely right.

Dr. S. A. Tea: In fact, on all of the questions you wrote in your own answer. For example, on the "running, swimming, bicycling" question you filled in, "My favorite sports are running, swimming, and dancing to Marilyn Manson."

On Identifying Sentence Errors and Improving Sentences questions, one out of five times there's no error.

Uboreme: Yeah, so?

Dr. S. A. Tea: You can't do that. The grammar sections are multiple-choice sections.

Uboreme: Freedom of speech, man.

Dr. S. A. Tea: Uboreme, the only freedom you will gain from filling in your own answers will be that of not attending college.

Uboreme: Funny, SAT man, so what do I need to do?

Dr. S. A. Tea: Uboreme, you are a "Megacorrector."

Uboreme: What's that?

Dr. S. A. Tea: You find something wrong with every question. What's important to realize is that when you are working on the *Identifying Sentence Errors* and *Improving Sentences* sections, one out of five times there is no error on any given question.

Uboreme: So, what should I do?

Dr. S. A. Tea: First, limit yourself to the multiple-choice answers. Secondly, don't Megacorrect. In other words, if you feel that there might be an error or there might not be an error, you are probably Megacorrecting and you should pick the "No Error" answer.

Improving Paragraphs

Dr. S. A. Tea: Now we move on to the final grammar section, which is called *Improving Paragraphs*.

Thor: Dr. Du-hude! First it was *Improving Sentences*, now it's *Improving Paragraphs,* what's next? *Improving Books*?

Dr. S. A. Tea: Calm down, Thor. This is the end. It doesn't get any bigger than *Improving Paragraphs.*

Uhhhhh: Big? Me big.

Dr. S. A. Tea: Thanks for sharing, Uhhhhh.

Gimme da ball, coach!

Here are the directions for the question type *"Improving Paragraphs"* as they have appeared on the College Board Web site.

<u>**Directions:**</u> ***Each of the following passages is an early draft of an essay. Some parts of the passages need to be rewritten.***

Read each passage and answer the questions that follow. Some questions are about particular sentences or parts of sentences and ask you to improve sentence structure and word choice. Other questions refer to parts of the essay or the entire essay and ask you to consider organization and development. In making your decisions, follow the conventions of standard written English. After you have chosen your answer, fill in the corresponding oval on your answer sheet.

Dr. S. A. Tea's Tips For "Improving Paragraphs"

1. Don't read the passage in depth. Skim through the passage so that you have a general idea of what the passage is covering.

2. After skimming the passage, go to the question area. Then go back and forth between the question area and passage, answering each question one at a time.

3. Once again, often you are looking for the basic errors we have spoken about: "matching," "vagueness," "hillbilly English," and "awkwardness."

Skim the passage; spend time on the questions.

4. Sometimes you will be asked about the organization or development of the passage. Just try to put things in the best possible "logical" order.

Practice Exercises

Before we do anything serious, let's have some fun. Here is a nonsensical passage about the non-existent "Giant Antarctic Howling Tarantula." Sort your way through the jokes and try to pick out the correct, serious answers. You are allowed to laugh at the jokes along the way. The answers and explanations can be found after the questions.

Improving Paragraphs Passage 1

(1) One of the world's rarest spiders is the Giant Antarctic Howling Tarantula (GAHT). (2) Nearly five inches in diameter, GAHTs are perhaps most distinctive because of the howling sound they constantly emit. (3) This howl, which one writer has described as a cross between a gestating timber wolf and Regis Philbin, is often heard during the mating season.

(4) GAHTs, the pranksters of the South Pole, enjoy nothing better than sneaking up on sleeping seals and scaring the bejesus out of them. (5) This is because in the Antarctic the temperature is unimaginably cold at night. (6) As a result, GAHTs have taken to sleeping in stacks at night to conserve energy.

(7) A GAHT has a unique way of hunting. (8) On a penguin or a seal it first hitches a ride to a small ice floe. (9) Then it dangles a few of its legs off the ice floe and wiggles them savagely. (10) With immaculate timing, the GAHT simultaneously yanks back its legs and swivels its head into the water, unleashing a powerful bite to the surprised fish.

(11) Once the venom and poison have been delivered to the fish, the GAHT must quickly pull the fish out of the water and onto the ice floe. (12) As the venom takes effect, the tarantula must dance around the exterior of the floe, constantly corralling the flopping fish to make sure that it doesn't leap off the floe and back into the water and into the ocean.

(13) The life of a Giant Antarctic Howling Tarantula would never be easy; in addition to the hardships of fishing in the frigid waters, these tarantulas must be always wary of the sky. (14) Albatrosses and petrels abound, and would like nothing better than an easy meal. (15) Only the occasional howl and perplexing question like, "Is that your final answer?" seem to keep these birds away.

1. Which of the following would be the most suitable sentence to insert in between sentence 4 and sentence 5?

A) Seals sometimes balance balls on their noses.

B) By early nightfall the tarantulas start to gather in herds.

C) After this, GAHTs gather to watch the game show *Who Wants to be a Millionaire?*

D) GAHTs are starting their own game show, *Who Wants a Few Extra Legs?*

E) Sometimes, in a similarly playful gesture, seals like to frighten GAHTs by eating them.

2. Which of the following versions is the best revision of sentence 8?

A) On a penguin or a seal it first sticks out its thumb to hitch a ride to a small ice floe

B) It hitches a ride on a floe to a penguin or a seal.

C) Oooh, penguins and seals are soooooh cute.

D) It hitches a ride on a penguin or a seal to a small ice floe.

E) It hitches a penguin to a seal and ices to the small floe.

3. Which of the following sentences would be best to place immediately after sentence 9?

A) What is all of this GAHT nonsense?

B) Poor little GAHT, wouldn't his toes get cold?

C) Did you know that GAHT spelled backwards is THAG? (Yes, Sireee, I have lots of time on my hands.)

D) GAHT ligs, hmmm. Now I et frog ligs and rabbet ligs, but I ain't never et GAHT ligs.

E) From a distance, fish mistake the tarantula for a squid or octopus and surge to the surface to attack.

4. Which of the following would be the best revision to the underlined portion of sentence 12?

As the venom takes effect, the tarantula must dance around the exterior of the floe, <u>constantly corralling the flopping fish to make sure that it doesn't leap off the floe and back into the water and into the ocean</u>.

A) (As it is now)

B) constantly corralling the ocean to make sure it doesn't flop back into the fish

C) constantly corralling the flopping fish to make sure it doesn't leap off the floe and go back into the ocean

D) constantly flopping the corral to make sure it doesn't go back into the ocean

E) constantly corralling the flopping fish to make sure the floe doesn't leap off back into the ocean

5. What would be the best revision of the underlined portion of sentence 13 reproduced below?

The life of a Giant Antarctic Howling Tarantula would never be easy; in addition to the hardships of fishing in the frigid waters, these tarantulas must be always wary of the sky.

A) (As it is now)

B) The life of a Giant Antarctic Howling Tarantula. Hey it's never easy

C) The life of a Giant Antarctic Howling Tarantula might could never be easy

D) The life of a Giant Antarctic Howling Tarantula is never easy

E) I want to be a Giant Antarctic Howling Tarantula

6. The function of sentence 15 is

A) to provide a roller coaster ending to this incredible, amazing saga.

B) to conclude the clear winner of the 2004 Pulitzer Prize for *Ridiculous Story about Imaginary Animals.*

C) to signal the clear prelude to a nuclear war.

D) to attempt one last lame joke.

E) a blatant attempt to land the author on the TV show *Live with Regis and Kelly.*

Answer key:
1) B   2) D   3) E   4) C   5) D
6) All answers are right.

EXPLANATIONS:

1) Answer (B) is right. Sentence 5 describes how cold it is in the Antarctic at night. Therefore a sentence introducing nightfall fits perfectly before sentence 5.

2) Answer (D) is right. This sentence is concise and grammatically correct. All of the other sentences are ridiculous.

3) Answer (E) is right. Sentence 9 describes how the GAHT lures its victims. Therefore, a sentence describing how fish fall for the bait is perfect.

4) Answer (C) is right. Only answer (C) is grammatically correct. All of the other sentences are farcical.

5) Answer (D) is right. Only answer (D) is grammatically correct. All of the other sentences are ludicrous.

6) All the answers are right and very, very wrong at the same time.

Wictoria: Great Wizard of the SAT, GAHTs are so cute! Where can I get a GAHT so I can get rid of the cat?

Dr. S. A. Tea: I hate to break it to you, Wictoria, but GAHTs are imaginary.

Okay, now it's time to get serious. Here's a second passage to practice with. Skim this passage and answer the questions. The answers and explanations to the answers follow the questions.

Improving Paragraphs Passage 2

(1) Today, many high school students have schedules that are even more strenuous than adults. (2) The life of Waisley Highsmith is a good example of many high school students' daily routine. (3) Waisley is a junior who plays water polo. (4) Water polo practice often is early; Waisley rises at 5 in the morning so that he can be at school by 6 a.m. to attend practice. (5) His team practices in the pool for nearly two hours and, after quickly showering, Waisley begins his school day at 8 a.m.

(6) School finishes at 3:00 p.m. and Waisley rushes back to the gym to switch into his bathing suit. (7) He swims laps from 3:30 to 5:30 p.m. and then goes home to have a quick dinner with his family. (8) After dinner Waisley usually attends an SAT preparation class or a student government meeting until 9 p.m. (9) Waisley really loves to play water polo. (10) When he returns home he spends an hour doing homework and then occasionally he finds time to relax for a half an hour before he goes to sleep around 11 p.m.

(11) Clearly, one thing that is lost with this is the opportunity for students like Waisley to have a normal night's sleep on a

regular basis. (12) Several studies have concluded that high students should sleep between eight and nine hours a night. (13) These studies suggest that a good night's sleep is crucial because constant sleep deprivation could prohibit proper brain development.

(14) So, let's add it up: some high school athletes like Waisley spend about $7\frac{1}{2}$ hours attending school and doing homework, 4 hours playing sports, and 2 hours attending evening meetings. (15) That adds up to about a $13\frac{1}{2}$ hour workday.

1. Of the following answers, which is the best revision of sentence 1 (reproduced below)?

A) (As it is now)

B) Today, many high school students have schedules that are even more strenuous than the schedules that adults might have.

C) Today, many high school students have schedules that are even more strenuous than those of adults.

D) Today, many high school students have schedules which when compared to the schedules of adults are even more strenuous.

E) Today, many high school students have schedules that make adults more strenuous.

2. To make paragraph 2 more coherent, which of the following sentences would be best to omit?

A) Sentence 6

B) Sentence 7

C) Sentence 8

D) Sentence 9

E) Sentence 10

3. Sentence 11 could be made more clear by adding which of the following sets of words after the word "this"?

A) moment

B) type of schedule

C) and that

D) is your life

E) is not fair

4. The purpose of paragraph 3 is to

A) to provide a reason why it is important to have a good bed

B) to contradict the rest of the passage

C) to state an effect of having an overburdened schedule

D) to discuss different sleeping positions

E) to glorify hard work

5. For the coherence of the passage, where is the best place for paragraph 4 to go?

A) Before paragraph 1

B) After paragraph 1

C) After paragraph 2

D) In the middle of paragraph 2 after line 7

E) After paragraph 3 (where it is now)

6. What might be a good sentence to add after sentence 15?

A) Buck up, dude. You aren't a man unless you work a 22-hour day.

B) But what does that have to do with the price of owls in Calcutta?

C) There's something I've been wondering about water polo: don't the horses drown sometimes?

D) What kind of freaky name is Waisley anyway?

E) This stands out in sharp contrast to the schedules of most adults, who work eight to nine hour days.

Conversation with Xasmine about extra credit on the SAT

Dr. S.A.Tea: Now the only problem here, Xasmine, is that there were just 20 questions on this section.

Xasmine: I know. Like I was so doing problem #21 for extra credit.

Dr. S.A.Tea: Xasmine, unfortunately there is no extra credit on the SAT, so if the section ends at question #20, you have to contain your answers to that number of questions.

Xasmine (whining): But, El Doctor, that is so-ooh unfair. I always get extra credit at school!

Answer key:
1) C   2) D   3) B   4) C   5) C
6) Okay, well it got a little silly here. (E) is
   probably the best straight answer.

EXPLANATIONS:

1) Answer (C) is right because it is the only one that makes a direct comparison between the schedules of high school students and the schedules of adults. Some of the other answers are wrong because they compare the <u>schedules</u> of the high school students to <u>people</u>, the adults, instead of comparing the <u>schedules</u> of the high school students to the <u>schedules</u> of the adults. In addition, the other answers are wrong because they are more awkward than the right answer.

2) Answer (D) is right because sentence 10 fits right after sentence 8. In other words, the passage is discussing Waisley's schedule. Sentence 9 interrupts the flow of the paragraph and would be the best one to eliminate.

3) Answer (B) is right because the word *this* refers back to the previous paragraph, which is a discussion of Waisley's schedule.

4) Answer (C) is right because so far the passage has been discussing Waisley's heavy schedule. Paragraph 3 then discusses the possible effects of having such a schedule.

5) Answer (C) is right because if paragraph 4 were placed immediately after paragraph 2, it would help the flow of the passage. Paragraph 4 is essentially summarizing the amount of hours that Waisley spends on different activities. This paragraph would fit perfectly after paragraphs 1 and 2 because these paragraphs list Waisley's activities.

6) Answer (E) is right because it offers a realistic comparison between Waisley's schedule and the schedule of an adult. Give yourself credit if you picked any of the other answers, though. At least you have a good sense of humor.

How did Thor score higher than me on anything?

What's Your Score?

Okay, now let's total it up. Give yourself one point for each answer you got right on the Waisley Highsmith passage.

If you scored . . .	
6 points	**When it comes to Improving Paragraphs, you da bomb!**
3-5 points	**When it comes to Improving Paragraphs, you maybe a cap gun!**
0-2 points	**I mean, I don't get it. Where is the "pair of graphs?"**

Tricks

In the Critical Reading and Math sections of the New SAT, we will be spending more time discussing how to avoid tricks. Since the essay is not a multiple-choice format, obviously there are no tricks on this section. However, on the grammar sections, there is one basic trick that the test makers use to fool you.

In the Introductory Area, we spoke about using your pop culture to help you learn vocabulary. In the Math section we will also discuss how your pop culture can help you with the math problems. However, in the grammar section, you should be wary of falling for tricks that revolve around phrases that you use in everyday language. For example, some songs use the lyrics "Just you and I." That is incorrect English. The correct phrase is "Just you and me." Another phrase that people use in everyday conversation is "I could care less." "I could care less" is incorrect

English. The correct phrase is "I couldn't care less." Think about it. If you say, "I could care less," you are saying that you **could** care less than you do.

The best way to avoid these types of tricks is to focus on formal English. You can be hip, just not on the SAT. You dig, dog?

YOU'RE DONE!

Congratulations! You have now finished the Writing section of the book. Next up, the Critical Reading section.

Critical Reading

The Critical Reading section on the New SAT will be most similar to the Verbal section on the Current SAT. The Verbal section on the Current SAT consists of three question types: **Reading Comprehension**, **Analogies**, and **Sentence Completions**.

The Critical Reading section on the New SAT will feature **Sentence Completions, Short Reading Passages,** and **Long Reading Passages.** The New SAT will no longer include **Analogies**.

The Permanent Effect of Working on Your Reading Ability

Let's forget the SAT for a minute. Why is it important to improve your reading ability?

1. Improving your reading ability can change your grades in high school. Think about it. Almost every subject in high school revolves around reading. If you improve your reading ability, you probably will find that school will become easier.

2. Improving your reading ability can change your grades in college. In just a few years you will be in college; if you haven't heard, the amount of reading you will be assigned in college likely will be much greater than what you are currently assigned in high school. You may be expected to read 500 to 1000 pages per week in college! If you can increase your reading speed and change your comprehension level, college will be a great deal easier.

3. Improving your reading ability can change the way you write, speak, and think. It's quite simple: Prolific readers are constantly absorbing huge amounts of information. If you can become a better reader you will not only improve your speaking and writing abilities, but you will also find that you have completely new ideas running through your head. You'll be a more interesting person!

Reading Section Overview

Dr. S. A. Tea: The name of the section we are dealing with here is Critical Reading.

Xasmine: Oh . . . my . . . God. Is the reading going to die?

Dr. S. A. Tea: Calm down, Xasmine. In this case, "critical" just means making an evaluation.

Xasmine: Phew, I was really worried!

Dr. S. A. Tea: Anyway, the point is that all three question types on the Critical Reading section involve reading comprehension.

Uhhhhh: Reading comprehension: What's dat?

Dr. S. A. Tea: Uhhhhh, let me break it down for you: One you don't do, the other you don't have.

Uhhhhh: Huh?

Dr. S. A. Tea: Never mind. Anyway, the point is that *Sentence Completions,* the *Short Reading Passages,* and the *Long Reading Passages* all test your ability to read. The main difference among these three types of reading is their length. *Sentence*

Completions are short tests of your reading ability, *Short Reading Passages* are medium tests of your reading ability, and *Long Reading Passages* are long tests of your reading ability.

Zino: Small, medium, and large — thatsa sounds like-a T-shirts.

Dr. S. A. Tea: That's a good analogy, Zino.

Uhhhhh: Small, medium, large . . . Dere's someding missing. I wear da extra-large T-shirt.

Dr. S. A. Tea: Uhhhhh, we're not talking about T-shirts, we're talking about the reading section! Now let's take a minute and talk about why the *Critical Reading* section is so difficult for many of you.

What's the Problem with the Reading Section?

Uboreme: SAT man, the reading is so utterly boring: Shantu, the mighty Bantu Warrior, the mating habits of the Tsetse fly . . . Why can't they have us read about something that's fun, like the blasted, bleak, barren landscape of a post-nuclear-war world?

Wictoria: Everything we read about is so real. Why can't we read about Harry Potter or Glinda, the good witch of the North?

Even if you find the reading boring, hang in there!

Dr. S. A. Tea: Enough with the wizards and witches already! The point is that you can't control what passages you will be assigned to read. You just have to deal with whatever they give you.

Xasmine: El Doctor, like why can't we do what we do when we don't want to read something for school.

Dr. S. A. Tea: What do you do?

Xasmine: Last year, for example, the teacher assigned us to read Dickens's *Great Expectations*. Like, I so fell asleep after the first paragraph. So then I was all let's go to the bookstore and I bought the *Tiny Notes So You Don't Have To Read* version of *Great Expectations*. Can I tell you, that book was almost as duh as the Dickens's book. I mean like I like the Dickens villages you can buy. I mean, awww, they're so pretty with the little shops and the snow and . . .

Dr. S. A. Tea, *cutting her off:* Okay, Xasmine, go on . . .

Xasmine: So I so rented the video, but, like, if you can believe this, the video was so ainchee, it was in black and white!

Dr. S. A. Tea: I hate to ask, but what is "ainchee"?

Ainchee?

Xasmine: El Doctor, get with it. "Ainchee" is ancient. Like, for example, "I can't go out with that guy. He's 24. Ewww. He's so ainchee!"

Dr. S. A. Tea: Thanks for clearing that up, Xasmine. Since many of you seem to be having trouble with the reading, let's go through some tips that should help you.

Dr. S. A. Tea's General Tips for the Critical Reading Section:

Tip

1. Realize that you actually have to read what you're given on the SAT. This isn't school. You can't have your friend read the book for you. You can't buy REA's *MAXnotes*® shortened version. You can't rent the video.

2. Concentrate. Whether you like the reading passages or not, the Critical Reading section counts for $1/3$ of your score on the New SAT. If you can get yourself to focus on the reading, you can completely change your overall score on the New SAT.

3. Determine the tone and main idea of what you are reading. For all three reading sections, if you can determine the general concept of what you are reading and the perspective of the writer, that will help you answer the majority of the questions.

Sentence Completions

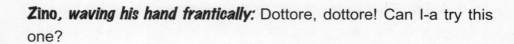

Dr. S. A. Tea: Let's start with the question type that has the shortest amount of reading: sentence completions. It's really very simple — all you have to do is fill in the blanks. Here's an example:

Tammy was very _____; however, her husband was a _____.

Zino, *waving his hand frantically:* Dottore, dottore! Can I-a try this one?

Dr. S. A. Tea: Sure, Zino.

Zino: Tammy was very warm; however, her husband was a-ugly.

Dr. S. A. Tea: What?

Xasmine: I think that Zino is trying to say that Tammy was hot; however, her husband was ugly.

Zino: Warm, hot, what-a-for the difference?

Dr. S. A. Tea: Let's start with the good news. Zino has spotted that the two blanks have an opposite relationship. There is only one minor problem. The sentence completion section is not a creative writing exercise; it actually is a multiple-choice section. So, it might be a good idea to actually look at the answers before making a guess. Here are the answers:

A) tall..dullard

B) intelligent..fool

C) wild..lunatic

D) amiable..sibling

E) tolerable..veteran

Zino: Oh, I-a get it. The answer issa (B).

Dr. S. A. Tea: Good job, Zino! Now, let's go over some quick tips for the easy *Sentence Completion* questions.

Dr. S. A. Tea's Tips for Easy Sentence Completions

1. Look for signal words that serve as clues to the direction of the sentence. For example, words like *but, however,* and *although* often turn around the direction of the sentence. Put another way, the blank will probably be opposite of some word or phrase that is already in the sentence.

Look for little words to tell you the direction of the sentence.

Example:

June was usually sweet, but today she was _____.

(In a case like this, you would be looking for an answer that would be opposite to the word *sweet:* for example, *mean*.)

On the other hand, a word like *similarly* or a pairing like *as...as* signifies that the blank is similar to a word or phrase that is already in the sentence.

Example:

The air was as clean as the water was _____.

(In a case like this, you would be looking for an answer that would be similar to the word *clean:* for example, *pure*.)

2. Focus on the most descriptive part of the sentence. Look for adjectives or vivid words.

Example:

The garden was a spectrum of brilliant colors; most people would say that the flowers were _____.

(What word catches your eye? Probably *brilliant,* right? Therefore, you would be looking for a word that would match up with *brilliant;* for example, the word *mesmerizing* might fit.)

3. If there are two blanks, notice the relationship between the blanks.

Example:

The storm was brutal: _____ and _____.

(In a case like this you would be looking for words that work together. For example, the answer would not be *rough* and *smooth*.)

4. Sometimes you can work on one blank at a time and make eliminations.

Example:

Far from _____ old difficulties, the program merely _____ new ones because it created different problems with deforestation.

A) fulfilling..reduced

B) propagating..made

C) eliminating..produced

D) elevating..irritated

E) annihilating..fixed

First of all, the answers in the two blanks are going to be opposite of each other. That is because of the phrase *far from*. In addition, if you substitute in all of the answers for the second blank, only answers (B) and (C) work. Now you only need to look at the first blank for answers (B) and (C). The first word for (C),

As long as you can eliminate answers, don't be afraid to guess.

eliminating, clearly works, so even if you don't know the meaning of the word *propagating,* you should go with answer (C). *Propagating* means "to reproduce or cause to spread," which means that (B) is a wrong answer.

5. Sometimes you may not know the right answer; instead, you may be able to eliminate several wrong answers.

Example:

Sally felt depressed much of the time, and her friends worried that she was too _____.

A) joyful

B) playful

C) morose

D) energetic

E) talkative

First of all, in this sentence, there is nothing that turns anything around. In other words, there are no words like but or however. Therefore, you are looking for a word that matches up with *depressed.* Clearly answers (A), (B), (D), and (E) don't work. The only answer left is (C), *morose. Morose* means "sad," but even if you didn't know the meaning of the word *morose,* you could get the right answer by eliminating all of the other answers that did not match up with *depressed.*

Practice Exercises

Now it's your turn. Here are a few easy sentence-completion questions to try. The answers and explanations follow the questions.

1. The special effects in "Terminator 2: Judgment Day" were groundbreaking at the time; they were truly_____.

A) awful

B) revolutionary

C) redundant

D) malodorous

E) hypocritical

2. The politician tried to present an image of consistency; even so, many of his statements seemed to _____ his past actions.

A) confirm

B) contradict

C) alleviate

D) bolster

E) anger

3. Wynton Marsalis has made his mark on the music world, impressing both the young and old; in fact, many argue that he is the _____ trumpeter of our time.

A) tallest

B) ancient

C) finest

D) laziest

E) slowest

4.   Because   Jim   is   both   _____   and _____, the teacher thinks that he is the best student in her class.

A) inane..ingenious

B) tawdry..jealous

C) lazy..malicious

D) inquisitive..clever

E) torpid..average

5. Though it has powerful legs, the sloth actually moves rather _____.

A) rapidly

B) angrily

C) violently

D) lethargically

E) intelligently

Answer key:
1) B   2) B   3) C   4) D   5) D

Gimme da coach, ball!

EXPLANATIONS:

1. The answer is (B). The most descriptive word in the sentence is *groundbreaking.* There is no word or phrase that turns the sentence around. Therefore, *revolutionary* is the best answer because it matches up best with *groundbreaking*.

2. The answer is (B). The most descriptive phrase in the sentence is *image of consistency*. The word *however* signifies that the sentence is going to be turned around. In this case you need to pick an answer that turns around the word *consistency.* Contradict is the best answer.

3. The answer is (C). One descriptive phrase is *made his mark* and one descriptive word is *impressing*. There is no word or phrase that turns the sentence around. Therefore, *finest* is the best answer because it matches up with *made his mark* and *impressing.*

4. The answer is (D). The most descriptive phrase in the sentence is *best student in the class.* Because there is no word or phrase that turns the sentence around, you are looking for an answer that matches up with *best student in the*

class. If you examine the answers in the second blank first, you can immediately determine that answers (B), (C), and (E) do not fit. If you look back at the first blank, clearly the word *inquisitive* fits. Even if you don't know the word *inane,* which means silly, you should pick answer (D) because the answers for both blanks fit the sentence.

5. The answer is (D). The most descriptive word in the sentence is *powerful.* The word *though* signifies that the sentence is going to be turned around. In this case you need to pick an answer that has an opposite effect of the word *powerful.* This time you may be forced to solve the question by means of elimination. Clearly, answers (A), (B), (C), and (E) are not the opposite of *powerful.* Even if you don't know the meaning of the word *lethargically,* you should pick answer (D) because all of the other answers don't work. *Lethargically* means "sluggishly," which in this case works as sort of an opposite to *powerful.*

Thor: Doctor Du-hude, as you quoite well know, I aced the Critical Reading section overall.

Dr. S. A. Tea: Yes, you did, Thor.

Thor: And when it came to the easy sentence-completion questions, I wasn't quoight sure if I could handle them. Yet, I very well did. However, the difficult questions are a whole different storrree.

Dr. S. A. Tea: That's a great point, Thor. Most of you will be able to solve the easy sentence completion questions. The issue will be handling the difficult questions. Here are some tips for handling the difficult sentence-completion questions.

Dr. S. A. Tea's Tips for Difficult Sentence Completions

1. Don't panic if you don't get all of the difficult sentence completion questions right. Until you have an incredible vocabulary, you are not going to get all of the difficult questions right. If you don't have an incredible vocabulary, your goal is to get <u>some</u> of the right answers on the difficult questions.

2. When you get to the difficult questions, first try to solve the problem yourself. If you are sure of an answer, you should go for it.

3. If you are not absolutely sure what answer to pick on a difficult question, try to avoid tricks. On the difficult sentence-completion questions, the answers that remind you too easily of the topic of the sentence often turn out to be tricks.

If you know the answer, go for it!

Example:

After scrutinizing the documents, the lawyers determined that in order to present an immaculate case, they would have to be _____ in court.

A) judgmental

B) impeachable

C) advisory

D) meticulous

E) legal

Answers (A), (B), (C), and (E) all sound like legal terms — things that you would associate with a lawyer. A test taker rushing through who is confused by this sentence would be likely to pick one of these answers. Instead, **the best answer is (D)**, *meticulous*. *Meticulous*, which means "being careful," matches up well with the words *scrutinize* and *immaculate*. *Scrutinize* means "to look at something carefully," and *immaculate* means "perfect." So, if you're faced with a difficult sentence completion question that is confusing, consider avoiding the trick answers that remind you too much of the topic.

4. If you're not sure of an answer on a difficult question, you should look for possible secondary meanings or metaphorical usage.

Example:

Deciding to focus on another project instead, the group opted to _____ the plans to build the new hockey arena.

A) table

B) detest

C) violate

D) emulate

E) defend

In a case like this, *table* would be the right answer. Many students would shy away from picking answer (A) because they

Conversation with Uboreme about his name

Dr. S.A.Tea: Uboreme, you have an interesting name. How did your parents decide to pick that particular name?

Uboreme: Actually, I picked my name.

Dr. S.A.Tea: How interesting! Tell me about that.

Uboreme: My parents left me unnamed until I was old enough to pick a name for myself.

Dr. S.A.Tea: And, how did you decide on Uboreme?

Uboreme: Well, originally I was going to call myself Youandtherestoftheworld boremetotearsIhateyouleave mealone, but that wouldn't fit into any of the school forms at school, so I shortened it to Uboreme.

Dr. S.A.Tea: Good idea.

think about the main definition of the noun *table* — "a piece of furniture." However, the verb *table* has other meanings. One definition of *table* used as a verb is "to put aside indefinitely." Secondary meanings are great tricks; in fact, the New SAT will likely have several questions with answers that feature secondary meanings.

5. If you're not sure of an answer on a difficult question, you can also consider picking a difficult word or pair of difficult words. The majority of test takers feel most comfortable picking words that they know. If your choice is between the word *stable* or the word *itinerant*, which word would you feel most comfortable picking? *Stable,* right? The test makers know that when you aren't sure of what the sentence is saying, you will tend to gravitate towards answers that have familiar words. That is why the answers on the difficult questions will often be difficult words.

6. The answers on the difficult questions will <u>not</u> always be the hardest words or possible secondary meanings. However, if you don't understand the sentence, picking a hard word or possible secondary meaning is a good guess. Once again, until you have an incredible vocabulary, don't expect to get every difficult sentence-completion question right. Your goal is to just get a good percentage of the answers right on the difficult questions.

7. Once again, when you get to the difficult questions, first try to solve the problem yourself. Even if you are on the most difficult sentence-completion question, if you know the answer, go for it. Don't even worry about looking for tricks if you know the answer.

Practice Exercises

Now it's your turn. Here are a handful of difficult-level sentence-completion questions for you to try. The answers and explanations follow the questions.

1. Professor Jones was a man who was _____; he was careful in his studies and thorough in his research.

A) exacting

B) elusive

C) absentminded

D) tangential

E) sibilant

2. Tubili, the conquerer, deliberately destroyed the most sacred buildings in the village; what the villagers had _____, Tubili completely _____.

A) consecrated..razed

B) vilified..ruined

C) worshipped..lauded

D) eliminated..annihilated

E) prized..resurrected

3. The night heron often stands motionless, waiting until an unwary fish is close enough to _____ and then _____.

A) attack..disgruntle

B) assail..devour

C) admire..conciliate

D) strike..avoid

E) alienate..consume

4. Normally the scientist would fall asleep or procrastinate before coming to the clinic, and her colleagues felt that she was _____.

A) banal

B) energized

C) languorous

D) laborious

E) experimental

5. Even though the two men had once shared a similar political perspective, a rift grew between them and their views _____.

A) tyrannized

B) dominated

C) desecrated

D) splintered

E) governed

Answer key:

1) A   2) A   3) B   4) C   5) D

EXPLANATIONS:

1) The answer is (A). *Exacting* means "being very careful." (Think about the word *exact*.) Answers like (C) and (D) are tricks because they are words that you often hear associated with professors and school.

2) The answer is (A). *Consecrated* means "worshipped," and *razed* means "destroyed." This answer works the best because Tubili <u>destroyed</u> the most <u>sacred</u> buildings. *Raze* is a very good trick word because it sounds like the word *raise*, which obviously has an opposite meaning.

3) The answer is (B). *Assail* means "to attack" and *devour* means "to eat." Many of the answers are tricks. For example, in addition to choice (B), choices (A) and (D) work for the first blank. The problem is that the second part of these answers does not work for the second blank.

4) The answer is (C). *Languorous* means "sluggish." Answer choices like (D) and (E) — in this case, words that you often hear associated with scientists — are tricks.

5) The answer is (D). In this case, *splintered* means "broken off from." This is a good example of a metaphorical use of a word. Normally, the word *splintered* refers to wood being

broken up into little pieces, but in this case the word *splintered* refers to the fact that the two men now have different political views. (A), (B), (C), and (E) are all tricks because they remind you too easily of the subject of politics.

What's Your Score?

Okay, now let's total your score from <u>both</u> the easy *Sentence Completion* questions and the difficult *Sentence Completion* questions. Give yourself one point for each answer you got right.

If you scored . . .

8-10 points   **You are the Master Sentence Completer!**

4-7 points   **You definitely _____ work on completing your _____.**

0-3 points   **Let's forget all about sentence completion, you need help with sentence conception!**

Long and Short Reading Passages

Uboreme: SAT man, please help me. I would rather put hot coals on my tongue than do any more of these reading passages!

Dr. S. A. Tea: Don't worry. Here are some tips on the reading passages that will make this section a good deal easier.

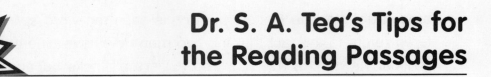

Dr. S. A. Tea's Tips for the Reading Passages

1. Even if you don't like to read, or you don't like a particular reading passage, force yourself to focus. The *Critical Reading* section is worth ¹/₃ of the entire test. How you score on the reading passages could conceivably determine which college you attend.

2. Try skimming the questions before you read the passage. Remember that your main goal is answering the questions correctly. For <u>some</u> students, skimming the questions before they read the passage is very effective. These students report that it helps them focus on important areas of the passage. Do not read the questions in depth. Just skimming the passages quickly should give you a good idea of what to look for in the passage.

3. The questions on the reading passages break down into two types: general and specific. <u>General questions</u> are things like "What's the main idea of the passage?" or "What would be a good title for the passage?" or "What's the tone of the passage?" <u>Specific questions</u> are questions like, "What does it mean when the author refers to 'candle in the wind' (line 25)?" or "In line 37, the word 'hole' most nearly means. . . ."

Try to get the main idea of the passage.

4. To determine the main idea of the passage and the perspective of the author, examine the first few lines and the last few lines of the passage. Whenever you read anything, you should always try to understand the overall concept and the opinion of the author. Think about it: Where do you put the most important information when you write an essay? The introduction and the conclusion, right? It's the same thing with reading passages. Usually the first few lines and the last few lines of the passage will explain the main idea of the passage and the perspective of the author. The beginning and end of the passage will often help you answer the general questions for the reading.

5. Don't skip over the italics that appear before the passage. Most likely only the longer reading passages will have italics. Sometimes the main idea of the passage or the opinion of the author appears in just these few lines.

6. When you are asked to define a vocabulary word, be careful not to fall for trick answers. First of all, if you are being asked to define a difficult vocabulary word and you actually know what the word means, go for the answer. However, if the answer fits too easily with the word, be careful.

Example:

In line 53, the word "chair" most nearly means

A) seat

B) follower

C) head

D) table

E) stool

If you haven't read the passage you might tend to pick an answer like (D), *table* or (E), *stool*. You might pick those answers because they remind you of the word *chair*. But now let's look at the word in context of the paragraph.

Conversation with Thor about the definition of multiple choice

Dr. S.A.Tea: Thor, I noticed that for some of the questions you filled in several answers.

Thor: Awl Roight, Doctor Du-hude. I was using the principle of multiple choice.

Dr. S.A.Tea: Thor, unfortunately I think that I need to redefine the concept of multiple choice for you. Multiple choice means that you get to pick between multiple answers, not that you get to put multiple answers on a single question.

Thor: Whoa, Doctor Du-hude. Thanks for clearing that up!

The student council elected a committee to handle the Prom. Herman was the chair of the committee. As the leader, he was in charge of making important decisions.

Now you can see why answers like (D) *table* or (E) *stool* are such good tricks. Be careful with questions that test vocabulary or phrases taken from the passage. Often the test makers will be trying to trick people who are too lazy to read the passage with obvious definitions.

7. To solve specific vocabulary questions, either try reading around the word for context, or use the *Dude, Check Out Their Answers* method. Remember the *Dude, Check Out Their Answers* method? This was the method Thor mentioned in the introductory area in which you check out the answers to solve the questions.

Let's look back at the problem we were just discussing.

In line 53, the word "chair" most nearly means

A) seat

B) follower

C) head

D) table

E) stool

Here is the piece of the passage we are examining:

The student council elected a committee to handle the Prom. Herman was the chair of the committee. As the leader, he was in charge of making important decisions.

There are two ways to solve this problem. Either you can read around the word *chair* so that you can make a guess as to the answer, or you can use the *Dude, Check Out Their Answers* method. All you have to do is substitute all of the answers for *chair*. If you make the substitutions, you will clearly see that answer (C) *head* works the best.

Wooscious!

8. If you know the meaning of a difficult vocabulary word, don't worry about tricks, just go for the answer.

Example:

In line 29, the word "misanthropic" most nearly means

A) one who hates mankind

B) one who loves mankind

C) one who is indifferent to mankind

D) one who likes women

E) one who likes animals

If you know that *misanthropic* means "one who hates mankind," you shouldn't worry about tricks and you should just pick answer (A).

Short Reading Passages

Okay, before we start the serious short reading passages, let's have some fun. Here is a short reading passage with an amusing twist. Read the passage and answer the questions that follow the passage. Try to pick out the serious answers, but you are allowed to laugh at the silly passage and answers. The answers and explanations follow the questions.

Short Reading Passage #1

"Jenkins, you fool. Stay away from the diving board!" I immediately decided to ignore Marlowe's suggestion. It was a humid summer night and I was enveloped in sweat. Sure, we'd all
Line heard rumors of the vicious beast that clambered into pools at
(5) night and disemboweled unwary swimmers. But, the heat was unbelievable. I bounced off the board, disregarding Marlowe's last cries. It seemed to take forever to reach the surface of the water, and then a blackness overtook me. Next, I remember waking up to excruciating pain in both of my arms and a face peering
(10) down at me, saying, "Jenkins, you fool! I tried to warn you; they drained the pool."

1. In line 3, "enveloped" most nearly means

A) stamped

B) sent

C) returned

D) covered

E) telephoned

2. The primary purpose of mentioning the "vicious beast" (line 4) is to

A) begin a discussion of endangered animals

B) examine the notion of predators in pools

C) highlight the strange relationship between Marlowe and the beast

D) clarify why the writer is named Jenkins

E) introduce a false lead before surprising the reader at the end of the passage.

Answer key:
1) D   2) E

EXPLANATIONS:

1. Answer (D) is the best answer. Try the *Dude, Check Out Their Answers* method. If you substitute in all of the answers, "I was covered in sweat," works the best. Answer (A), (B), and (C) are all tricks because they remind you too much of *envelope*.

2. Answer (E) is the best answer. The beast is introduced as a distraction. The reader is led to believe that the beast is the reason why Marlowe is warning Jenkins not to jump into the pool. This sets up the surprise ending where it is clear that the problem is not a beast but a drained pool.

Conversation with Wictoria about reincarnation

Dr. S.A.Tea: I understand you have some interesting thoughts about the afterlife.

Wictoria: Absolutely. Like sometimes when I concentrate on a spell there will be a fly buzzing around the room, and I think about how the fly might actually be the reincarnation of Bruce Willis.

Dr. S.A.Tea: That's quite fascinating; however, Bruce Willis is still alive.

Wictoria: Oh... well in my coven we believe that you can be reincarnated before you die.

Zino: Count S. A. Tea, I vant to tellll you, that vas classicallll!

Dr. S. A. Tea, *looking at the class:* Translation?

Thor, *sighing:* Zino's now in vampire mode and he's trying to say, "That's classic."

Okay, now that we've had some fun, let's get down to business. Here are two serious short reading passages. Read the first passage and then answer the questions. The answers and explanations follow the questions.

Short Reading Passage #2

　　　　When most people think of music in the 1970s, disco comes to mind. One of the decade's most vivid pictures is John Travolta in a white suit, strutting to the pounding rhythm of the
Line Bee Gees. However, the 1970s produced many other important
(5) forms of music. Artists like Steely Dan, Earth, Wind & Fire, and Stevie Wonder created a fusion of rock, funk, and jazz. In this new music, horn sections were featured prominently, and saxophonists and guitarists played extended, intricate solos. Sure, when it's "70s" night at a high school, the disc jockeys break out
(10) *Saturday Night Fever*, but the 1970s was also a time of creation for many different wonderful new forms of music besides disco.

1. The author's main point in the passage is to

A) emphasize the importance of disco in the 1970s

B) demonstrate that other forms of music besides disco were created in the 1970s

C) describe the importance of appearance and dancing in the 1970s

D) discuss the mysterious disappearance of jazz in the 1970s

E) reveal how disco metamorphosed into jazz in the 1970s

2. The phrase "created a fusion" in line 6 most nearly means

A) banishing unnecessary elements

B) harnessing atomic energy

C) making trouble

D) producing a meld

E) forcing a conflict

Answer key:
1) B   2) D

EXPLANATIONS:

1) (B) is the right answer. Although the author begins the passage by mentioning the staying power of disco, the primary purpose of this passage is to discuss the other new forms of music created in the 1970s. This is reinforced by the final sentence of the paragraph.

2) Answer (D) is the right answer. Try the *Dude, Check Out Their Answers* method. If you substitute in all of the answers, *producing a meld* of "rock, funk, and jazz," works the best. If you don't know, *meld* means "mix."

Okay, ready for the third short reading passage? Remember the tips, read the passage, and answer the questions.

Short Reading Passage #3

We are in a rapidly shifting culture. Whereas twenty years ago almost every intelligent person read books and newspapers, today many young people only read printed material when they
Line are forced to study for school. While this drop in interest in read-
(5) ing is deplorable, it is crucial to realize that we are in a changing culture. With the advent of a more video-oriented culture, teenagers now have many more choices than did previous generations. The Internet, cable TV, and portable game players are just some of the options that many teenagers are turning to. In the future,
(10) society's educators will have to continue to adapt their teaching methods to more video-oriented media if they want to continue to encourage the growth of young people's intelligence.

1. The word "advent" as used in line 6 most nearly means

A) abandoning

B) coming

C) freezing

D) talking

E) stopping

2. According to the passage, what will "society's educators" have to do to attract the attention of young people?

A) Hang out at a street corner and yell at them

B) Buy expensive TVs

C) Watch *South Park*

D) Change their teaching styles to include more video-oriented media

E) Paste books to the screens of computers

Answer key:

1) B　2) D

EXPLANATIONS:

1) (B) is the right answer. Use the *Dude, Check Out Their Answers* method. Just plug in answer (B) and you will see that "with the **coming** of a more video-oriented culture" clearly works the best.

2) (D) is the right answer. Obviously some of these answers are jokes. Answer (D) is reemphasized in the final sentence of the paragraph.

What's Your Score?

Okay, now let's total your score from <u>both</u> of the serious Short Reading Passages.

If you scored . . .	
3 or 4 points	**Master of the Short Reading Passage**
1 or 2 points	**Dude! This was only a 100-word passage. Hang in there.**
0 points	**Let's try this one: "See Spot run . . . "**

Long Reading Passages

Okay, before we start the serious long reading passages, let's have some fun. Here is a passage that presents an interesting "theory" about dinosaurs. Read the passage and answer the questions that follow the passage. Try to pick out the serious answers, but you are allowed to laugh at the silly passage and answers. The answers and explanations follow the questions.

Long Reading Passage #1

The following passage presents a theory that explains why dinosaurs disappeared from the Earth.

Approximately 65 million years ago, dinosaurs suddenly disappeared from the Earth. Throughout the years many theories

have been espoused, but one popular theory suggests that a
meteor hit the Earth with such velocity that the atmosphere and
living conditions were changed so irreparably that dinosaurs
could no longer survive.

But if all of the dinosaurs died because of a meteor hitting
the Earth, why have so few fossils been found? Modern humans
have only existed for thousands of years, yet the age of the
dinosaurs lasted millions of years. Surely there must have been
millions, if not billions, of dinosaurs who lived during this time
period. Where are all of their bones?

Some scientists would claim that many of the fossils are
still buried under the Earth or lay deep within the ocean. Other
researchers might state that many of the bones have disinte-
grated or been eaten by other animals. These theories seem to
me to be too simplistic, too pedestrian.

First, let's start with an assumption that I believe has been
too easily made. Those who promote the meteor theory most
certainly believe that dinosaurs had no warning that the meteor
was going to hit the Earth, and therefore no foreshadowing of
their doom. This is to me is a grave error. Clearly, what these
scientists have overlooked is a built-in warning system: dinosaurs
with long necks. A dinosaur such as Brachiosaurus could have
easily seen the approaching meteor well before it hit the Earth.
But at this point, you say, "That's preposterous. Brachiosaurus
died off nearly 100 million years before the rest of the dinosaurs
became extinct." My answer to this objection is simple: come on,
let's not quibble over small details.

Then you ask, "Even if some of the dinosaurs had seen the
meteor as it hurtled towards the Earth, what could they have done?"
The answer seems crystal clear to me: the dinosaurs could have
built spaceships and escaped from the Earth before the meteor
hit.

(35)   "But," you scoff, "that's ridiculous. First, how could dinosaurs build spaceships without materials such as aluminum and titanium? Second, how would the dinosaurs have harnessed enough power to leave the Earth? Finally, once in outer space, what fuel could they possibly have used?"

(40)   The answers to these questions are devastatingly simple. First, even though materials like aluminum and titanium were not available to dinosaurs, there was plenty of wood. Think about every movie you have ever seen about dinosaurs. They are always crashing through some kind of forest. A dinosaur such as

(45) Brachiosaurus could have easily toppled a few trees. Then it would have merely taken some raptors with sharp teeth to fashion these trees into spaceships.

       "Okay," you say, "but what about harnessing enough power to leave the Earth?"

(50)   This problem, my friend, caused me many sleepless nights. At first I entertained the possibility that the dinosaurs could have employed a "thrust" method for liftoff; perhaps several dinosaurs with strong shoulders and backs like Triceratops and Styracosaurus positioned each spaceship on their shoulders and

(55) then shoved the spaceships off the ground. However, after some careful consideration, it was clear that by using the "thrust" method alone, the dinosaurs would have been able to heave the spaceship only a few feet into the air.

       Next, I considered the "push" possibility. Perhaps the

(60) spaceships had been built with large holes in their bottoms. This would have allowed some of the dinosaurs to stand with their feet firmly planted on the ground. If several dinosaurs with strong legs, such as Tyrannosaurus Rex, had pushed at the same time, perhaps this might have propelled the rockets into space. How-

(65) ever, after further calculations, I determined that even the "push" method would not have been enough in itself to launch the dinosaur spaceships into space. By the way, at this point some of you

may say, "Aha! Here's another problem with your theory. If the spaceships had holes in the bottom and therefore were not air-
(70) tight, how would the dinosaurs have survived in the vacuum of space?" This query is easy to dismiss. Dinosaurs had huge lungs. It would have been very easy for a dinosaur to take a deep breath and hold it until, say, Mars.

One night, after I had been struggling with this problem for
(75) weeks, the answer suddenly hit me. The dinosaurs must have used a "thrust and push" method. While dinosaurs such as Triceratops and Styracosaurus used their shoulders and backs to thrust, a dinosaur like Tyrannosaurus Rex was simultaneously pushing with its feet. If the dinosaurs had coordinated these ef-
(80) forts with a "on the count of three," I am sure that they could have mustered the necessary energy to propel the spaceships into space.

"Okay," you say, "But what about the fuel needed to fly the spaceship through space?"
(85) The answer to this last question is a perfect example of overlooking the obvious. Where do we get our fuel today? From dinosaurs! Sure, it must have been difficult for dinosaurs to rocket through space knowing that their fuel was "Great Aunt Betty," however I am sure that all was done in the most urgent sense of
(90) survival. No matter how great the sacrifice, imagine the pride of the first dinosaur that touched down on a distant planet and roared, "One small step for a dinosaur, one giant step for the Dinokind."

1. In line 3, the word "espoused" most nearly means

A) an Internet husband

B) an Internet wife

C) promoted

D) having the power to read others' thoughts. . . . uh. . . . oused

E) No more lame jokes, please, I beg you!

2. The purpose of the first paragraph is

A) to present the only piece of sanity within this article

B) to create an illusion that the article should be taken seriously

C) to make you forget all about the Great Antarctic Howling Tarantula

D) to introduce a popular scientific theory about dinosaurs

E) to introduce a popular dinosaur theory about scientists

3. In line 17, the word "pedestrian" most nearly means

A) a man crossing a street

B) a woman crossing a street

C) a baby crawling across a street

D) a target for drivers in New York City

E) common

4. The main purpose of this passage is:

A) to demonstrate how crazy the writer is

B) to demonstrate how crazy you are for reading this

C) to make you want to build your own spaceship out of wood

D) to reevaluate your old view of Tyrannosaurus Rex as a vicious brute and perhaps realize that this animal was a hard worker that was willing to do anything to help get the space-ship off the ground

E) to present a new theory about dinosaurs

5. The tone of lines 68 to 73 (about dinosaurs holding their breath) can best be categorized as

A) humorous

B) lame

C) with all the sitcom writers laid off because of the Reality TV craze, this is the best you could do for humor?

D) an advertisement for an airplane "sick" bag

E) Dinomite (why, oh why, did you just make that joke?)

6. A good title for this passage might be:

A) Dinosaurs: Friends and Astronauts

B) Dinosaurs: They didn't go extinct; they built spaceships and left Earth

C) Why some writers shouldn't be given a voice

D) The Dinokind: When will they return?

E) The strange relationship of Bill Clinton and the Iguanadon

Answer key:
1) C   2) D   3) E   4) E   5) A   6) take your pick

EXPLANATIONS:

(Remember again, these were the "serious" answers)

1) (C) is right. Try the *Dude, Check Out Their Answers* method. If you substitute *promoted* for *espoused,* you will see that it fits perfectly.

2) (D) is right. In the first paragraph, the author introduces a popular theory for the extinction of dinosaurs: the meteor theory.

3) (E) is right. Try the *Dude, Check Out Their Answers* method. If you substitute *common* for *pedestrian,* you will see that it fits perfectly. The word *pedestrian* is also a good example of a word that has several meanings. As we discussed earlier in the *Sentence Completion* section, using secondary meanings is one of the test maker's greatest tricks.

4) (E) is right. After the first paragraph, the author spends the rest of the passage explaining his harebrained theory.

5) (A) is right. The tone of this part of the passage technically qualifies as humorous.

6) Any answer is fine.

Zino: Doctor Dead, that passage was red.

Dr. S. A. Tea: Huh?

Thor, *sighing*: Let me translate. Zino is trying to say, "Doctor Du-hude, that passage was rad."

Dr. S. A. Tea: The sad thing is that I'm starting to understand Thor.

Okay, now that we've had some fun, let's get down to business once again. Here are two serious reading comprehension passages. Read the first passage and then answer the questions. The answers and explanations follow the questions.

Long Reading Passage #2

In this passage, an American writer describes the town where she spent her childhood.

In this hectic, technology-laden world, it is increasingly difficult to find a place of refuge and good, old-fashioned values. I suppose I am lucky because I grew up in a small town where life
Line slows down and people still greet you by name on the street.
(5)   Tucked into the western corner of New York state on the edge of Lake Erie, Westfield is a haven where everyone knows everyone else and folks still tend to leave their doors unlocked at night. Young and old alike revel in the time-tested pursuits of walking down Main Street licking an ice cream cone from the

(10) local Tasty Freeze and dressing up for a night of Halloween fun. Yes, in Westfield, Halloween still takes place at night, and trick-or-treaters go door to door, not from supermarket to hardware store as now happens in many suburban areas. For all its home-grown fun, even a town like Westfield does not want for culture. **(15)** Everyone enjoys concerts of all musical genres in the town gazebo during the summer months and acclaimed lecturers at the library on frosty winter afternoons.

     A town that is geographically small provides an immense playground for kids. As a child, my bike could take me anywhere I **(20)** wanted to go in my hometown. I perfected the art of riding without hands all the way back to my house from the public recreational park, where I had swimming and arts and crafts lessons on summer mornings. It was common for kids to walk down to Chautauqua Gorge for a fossil-hunting expedition along the creek **(25)** during fall's multi-hued splendor. When the wind wafted just right, you could hear the whack of the diving board and elated squeals from almost anywhere in town as yet another child was inducted into the joys of the deep end at the Welch Field pool. Every Friday night, the roller skating soirée at Eason Hall attracted kids **(30)** from all the neighboring towns.

     Established in 1802, my town was at a strategic crossroads on the Portage Trail. Now an important road, this trail was originally used by local Native Americans, and later French trappers, to portage their canoes from Lake Erie up the hill to Lake **(35)** Chautauqua. Westfield is also not without its famous residents. William Seward, the Secretary of State under President Lincoln and the man responsible for the purchase of Alaska, built his mansion in Westfield. A precocious innocent by the name of Grace Bedell was also connected to Abraham Lincoln, and she **(40)** wrote to him suggesting that he grow a beard. Our sixteenth president took to the idea and to little Grace, stopping to see her when his Presidential train rode through the town en route to the White House.

(45) My hometown retains its Victorian charm while still maintaining present-day relevance. In Westfield, one is able to bridge the gap between old and new. It is a place where the attitudes of yesteryear co-exist with the forward thinking spirit of today. Isn't it nice that one can still have a slice of tranquility with a topping of unabashed fun in this digital age?

1. The author's perspective towards Westfield is one of

A) nonchalance

B) irritation

C) indifference

D) fondness

E) disbelief

2. In line 8, the word "revel" most nearly means

A) make clear

B) fight against authority

C) take pleasure

D) unveil

E) amplify

3. The primary purpose of paragraphs 2 and 3 is to emphasize

A) the benefits of an old-fashioned small town

B) the constrictions of living in a small town

C) the advantages of celebrating Halloween at night

D) the freedom of living near a gorge

E) the danger of living in a town where doors are unlocked at night

4. The main purpose of paragraph 4 is to

A) describe the intricacies of the Portage Trail.

B) discuss why Lincoln grew a beard

C) demonstrate the historical importance of Westfield

D) reveal Lincoln's connection to Westfield

E) establish the strange connection between Seward and Lincoln's beard

5. In lines 45-46, "bridge the gap" most nearly means

A) connecting the two sides of the Chautauqua Gorge

B) bringing together

C) going to buy jeans

D) filling in the space between teeth

E) connecting the Tasty Freeze to Welch Field

Answer key:
1) D   2) C   3) A   4) C   5) B

EXPLANATIONS:

1) The answer is (D). Throughout the passage the writer speaks positively of Westfield. For example, the second line of the passage reads, "I suppose I am lucky because I grew up in a small town where life slows down and people still greet you by name on the street." The writer clearly enjoyed growing up in Westfield and throughout the rest of the passage speaks of her town with glowing adjectives and metaphors.

2) The answer is (C). Try the *Dude, Check Out Their Answers* method. If you substitute in all of the answers for the word *revel*, "take pleasure" fits the best. The other answers are either neutral or negative words.

3) The answer is (A). "The benefits of an old-fashioned small town" is clearly the theme of the passage. Paragraphs 2 and 3 bolster this theme with specific examples. Although answers (C) and (D) are mentioned as positive aspects of living in Westfield, neither answer serves as the <u>primary</u> purpose of paragraphs 2 and 3.

4) The answer is (C). The Portage Trail, Lincoln, and Seward are mentioned to demonstrate the historical significance of

Westfield. Although (A), (B), and (D) are all mentioned in this paragraph, none of them serve as the overall, <u>main</u> purpose of the paragraph.

5) The answer is (B). Try the *Dude, Check Out Their Answers* method. If you substitute in all of the answers for *bridge the gap*, the phrase *bringing together* works the best. The trick here is to realize that *bridge* is being used in a metaphorical sense. In other words, there is no actual bridge, it's as if there were a bridge.

Let's try one last passage. Read the passage and answer the questions. The answers and explanations follow the questions.

Long Reading Passage #3

Charlayne Hunter-Gault was the first African-American woman to be accepted to the University of Georgia. This passage discusses Ms. Hunter-Gault's struggle for admission to the University of Georgia and the significance of her participation in the Civil Rights movement of the 1950s and 1960s in the United States.

In 1959, the civil rights leaders of Atlanta were trying to figure out how to bring civil rights activism to Georgia. Influenced by the successful, though contentious, desegregation of Little
Line Rock High School in Arkansas, the Atlanta Committee for Coop-
(5) erative Action (ACCA) decided to try and test the practice of continued, illegal college segregation at the University of Georgia. The committee needed an eligible, African-American student who had an unblemished background and character. An aspiring journalist from Atlanta, Charlayne Hunter-Gault, was chosen as a
(10) test case.

The desegregation of the nation's schools and universities was an integral part of the civil rights movement in the 1950s and 1960s. Young and eager to succeed in life, Charlayne Hunter-Gault became an important player in this struggle. She was hon-
(15) ored that the ACCA had selected her to try to break the racial barrier at the University of Georgia. However, Hunter-Gault's battle began in earnest when she was unceremoniously denied admission to the school after she submitted her first application.

On December 13, 1960, Charlayne Hunter-Gault attended
(20) a trial in Athens, Georgia, to determine why she had been denied admittance to the University of Georgia. Despite her youth, she understood the significance of that winter morning. Her rejection from the University of Georgia was one of the top news stories in the country, and the entire nation had turned its eyes to this
(25) corner of the South to see what would happen to this intelligent and gifted African-American girl. Hunter-Gault had a plethora of lawyers, civic leaders, and civil rights activists in her camp, all fighting for her rightful instatement in the University of Georgia. She was struggling for something that had been wrongfully de-
(30) nied her and anyone else that a select group of white people classified as "unacceptable." She was an ideal student and up-standing citizen with definite plans and future aspirations, all aspects that universities look for in their students. But, she was black. It was this "but" that Hunter-Gault was protesting by at-
(35) tempting to gain admission to the University of Georgia.

In January of 1960, Hunter-Gault learned that she had finally been admitted to Georgia for the spring quarter. When she arrived back in her hometown of Atlanta, Hunter-Gault received plaudits from her fellow African Americans. They were proud of
(40) her and through her they could see that their time for justice was at hand. Hunter-Gault gained confidence through their smiles and congratulations, which helped to soothe her fears concerning her

groundbreaking course of action. However, her success was short-lived. When Hunter-Gault took up residence at the Univer-
(45) sity of Georgia to begin her education, she was removed from the school after mobs incited violent demonstrations outside her dormitory.

Unfortunately, Hunter-Gault endured a difficult period when she was alternately removed and then reinstated at the University
(50) of Georgia. After she was finally reinstated at the university once and for all, due in large part to faculty petitions, Hunter-Gault went about her studies but confronted racism head on whenever it revealed itself. While many students were initially upset about her presence in their classrooms and dorms, Hunter-Gault ob-
(55) served that her presence grew on people. She provided a face and name to the ambiguous label of "black," and many white students soon befriended Charlayne the person instead of just seeing Charlayne the African American. Hunter-Gault labored to highlight the fact that she was a student just like other students.
(60) She strived to show that she was no different than white students who were pursuing the same education she was working so hard for.

In her quest to overcome the collegiate racial barrier, Hunter-Gault continually underlined the importance of under-
(65) standing her fellow white students. Hunter-Gault was undeniably very proud of her accomplishments as a black woman, but she was perhaps even more proud of the fact that she was able to highlight the shared connections between whites and blacks on the academic level. Hunter-Gault grasped the significance that,
(70) for many whites, uncovering these connections rendered the goals of civil rights less intolerable and more understandable and effective. The fact that a black woman was enrolled at a previously all-white university showed that change was inevitable, and that it could come in many forms, including the intelligent, young,
(75) innocent yet eager personality of Charlayne Hunter-Gault.

1. According to the passage, the ACCA decided to test college segregation at the University of Georgia because

A) other countries had abolished segregation years before

B) private colleges in Georgia had already admitted African-American students

C) Little Rock High School had recently been desegregated

D) Hunter-Gault had been accepted at many other colleges across the country

E) other African-American students had already been accepted at the University of Georgia

2. In line 17, the phrase "unceremoniously denied" most nearly means

A) rejected without any special explanation

B) not given a regal coronation

C) disallowed visiting privileges

D) fooled by documents

E) cancelled indefinitely

3. The "significance of that winter morning," mentioned in line 22, refers to the fact that

A) Hunter-Gault experienced the coldest day in Atlanta's history

B) Hunter-Gault's trial would likely have a more far-reaching effect on all African Americans

C) this particular winter morning was the first day that the ACCA office opened

D) a decision on the trial might occur at any moment

E) lawyers, civic leaders, and civic right activists all had decided to offer their assistance to her on this one particular day

4. In line 34, the "but" that Hunter-Gault was protesting refers to the fact that she was

A) admitted to the University of Georgia, but subsequently removed

B) admitted to the University of Georgia, but was not offered a scholarship

C) qualified to apply to the University of Georgia, but not approached by the ACCA

D) qualified to be admitted to the University of Georgia, but had been rejected because of her race

E) rejected by the University of Georgia and subsequently admitted

5) In line 39, the word "plaudits" most nearly means

A) pleas

B) compensation

C) complaints

D) stares

E) praise

6) In line 43, in context the phrase "groundbreaking course of action" refers to the fact that Hunter-Gault was

A) tunneling through enemy lines

B) taking a new course at the University of Georgia in seismology

C) helping to build new houses in her neighborhood

D) becoming the first woman to attend the University of Georgia

E) becoming the first African-American woman to attend the University of Georgia

7) According to the passage, Hunter-Gault attempted to surmount the collegiate racial barrier

A) by spending many hours studying for her classes

B) by working to understand her fellow white students

C) by working off campus and getting to know the people in her neighborhood

D) by attending trials of other African-American students who had been wrongfully denied admission to universities

E) by apprenticing for the ACCA during the summer

8) In line 56, the word "ambiguous" most nearly means

A) able to use both hands

B) miserable

C) able to exist in land and water

D) unclear

E) violent

9) The author would consider which of these statements to be FALSE?

A) Hunter-Gault worked hard to stay at the University of Georgia

B) One of the reasons why the ACCA picked Hunter-Gault was because of her character

C) Hunter-Gault segregated herself from white students in order to avoid problems

D) Hunter-Gault's admission was important for many young African-American students

E) Until Hunter-Gault's admission, the University of Georgia had not admitted any African Americans

10) The tone of the author can best be characterized as

A) jovial

B) angry

C) miserable

D) factual

E) harsh

Answer key:

1) C   2) A   3) B   4) D   5) E   6) E   7) B   8) D
9) C   10) D

EXPLANATIONS:

1. (C) is right. In the first paragraph, it clearly states that the ACCA decided to test college segregation at the University of Georgia because Little Rock High School in Arkansas had been successfully desegregated.

2. (A) is right. Try the *Dude, Check Out Their Answers* method. If you substitute all of the answers, "rejected without any special explanation" best fits the sentence. Also, in the first sentence of the third paragraph, the passage states that Hunter-Gault decided to go to trial against the University of Georgia because she was rejected from the school.

3. (B) is right. The "significance" is that this trial would likely

have more far-reaching effects. Later in the paragraph, the author writes that "the entire nation had turned its eyes to this corner of the South to see what would happen to this intelligent and gifted African-American girl."

4. (D) is right. Just a few sentences before the "but," the author writes that Hunter-Gault was "an ideal student and upstanding citizen with definite plans and future aspirations. . . . But she was black." Then the author definitively states that, "It was this 'but' that Hunter-Gault was protesting by attempting to gain admission to the University of Georgia. . . . "

5. (E) is right. Try the *Dude, Check Out Their Answers* method. By simple substitution the phrase "Hunter-Gault received **praise** from her fellow African Americans" fits the best.

6. (E) is right. Throughout the passage, the author reiterates that Hunter-Gault was the first African American woman to be accepted to the University of Georgia. Earlier, in the first line of the same paragraph that contains the phrase "groundbreaking course of action," the author states that, "Hunter-Gault learned that she had finally been admitted to the University of Georgia."

7. (B) is right. All you need to do is to read the entire sentence (line 63), "In her quest to overcome the collegiate racial barrier, Hunter-Gault continually underlined the importance of understanding her fellow white students."

8. (D) is right. Try the *Dude, Check Out Their Answers* method. If you substitute in all of the choices, "She provided a face and a name to the *unclear* label of 'black'" fits the best.

Conversation with Xasmine about her extraordinarily "tall" platform sandals

Dr. S.A.Tea: Xasmine, I know that platform sandals are all the rage right now, but your sandals seem to be extraordinarily tall. How tall are the platforms?

Xasmine: Eight and a half inches.

Dr. S.A.Tea: Eight and a half inches! Aren't they cumbersome?

Xasmine: Oh, no. These are my lucky sandals. I met Justin Timberlake wearing these sandals and he took me right into his arms.

Dr. S.A.Tea: That must have been exciting for you. So, Justin Timberlake gave you a hug?

Xasmine: No, I tripped and he caught me.

9. (C) is right. Towards the end of the passage, the author goes to great lengths to state that Hunter-Gault took great pride in understanding white students and interacting with them.

10. (D) is right. The author's style is factual. She relates Hunter-Gault's history and then discusses the effect of Hunter-Gault's admission to the University of Georgia. On the other hand, all of the other answers express some sort of emotion that is not found in this passage.

What's Your Score?

Okay, now let's total up your score from <u>both</u> of the serious Long Reading Passages. Give yourself one point for each answer you got right.

If you scored	
12-15 points	Master of the Long Reading Passage
5-11 points	Let's learn a new word: "library"
0-4 points	Hint: you're holding this book upside down

You're Done!

Congratulations! You have now finished the Critical Reading section of the book. Next up, the Math section.

Math

4

The Math section of the New SAT will be fairly similar to the Math section of the Current SAT. The Current SAT has three question types: **Multiple-Choice**, **Quantitative Comparison**, and **Student-Produced Responses.** The New SAT will drop the **Quantitative Comparisons** and will have just two Math question types: **Multiple-Choice Items** and **Student-Produced Responses**. The Math section on the New SAT will also include some Algebra II-level questions for the first time.

The Permanent Effect of Working on Your Math Ability

Let's forget the SAT for a minute. Why is it important to improve your math and logic skills?

1. Improving your math ability can change your grades in high school. If you can improve your reasoning ability and cut down on careless errors, you will most likely improve your math grade in school. Also, remember that much of science is math-related; working on your math ability could affect your science grades as well.

2. Improving your math ability can change your grades in college. Even if you are going to major in a non-math-related field in college, you will likely have to take at least one math and one science course. If you can't handle Algebra I or Geometry, what are you going to do if you have to take Pre-Calculus or Calculus?

3. Improving your math ability can change your financial situation in life. Let's face it, for many of you math has one major connection to life: MONEY. If you don't have a good feel for basic numbers or calculations now, you may have reduced your potential for achievements later in life. For example, maybe you won't negotiate the best deal for yourself when you buy a car, or maybe you won't make the wisest decisions when you're trying to invest in the stock market or real estate.

Math Section

Dr. S. A. Tea: Okay, who's worried about the Math section of the New SAT?

Zino: Daaktar, please to help me. I em wurrying about dees Myth section all de time. I mean when I em a young man, day efter every day I em learning about Greek Myths, Roman Myths, Norse Myths, Hindi Myths. . . .

Dr. S. A. Tea: Math, Zino, not Myths!

Zino: Oh! I em thanking you very much for clearing up dat mud puddle en my mind.

How Will the Math Section Change for the New SAT?

The College Board has stated that the New SAT will include concepts from Algebra II for the first time. However, it is unlikely that the New SAT will be dominated by Algebra II questions. There will still be many Algebra I and Geometry questions.

In addition, the College Board has also released a list of the new types of concepts that MAY be tested on the New SAT. Here is just a quick list of some of these concepts:

Number and Operations concepts

Example: Population Growth questions

Additional Algebra concepts

Example: Absolute Value and Radical Equations questions

Additional Geometry and Measurement Concepts

Example: Questions involving 30:60:90 and 45:45:90 triangles in which Trigonometry can be used as an alternate method of solution

Additional Data Analysis, Statistics, and Probability Concepts

Examples: Questions involving Data Interpretation, Scatterplots, and Matrices (essentially analyzing charts)

What Does All of that Mean?

Essentially, the Math section on the New SAT will still include logic and reasoning questions that appeared on the Old SAT. However, the math on the New SAT will also include questions that are more technical. In other words, some questions may rely more heavily on formulas and calculator usage.

We're Not Going to Cover Every Little Detail of Geometry, Algebra I and Algebra II

The purpose of this book is to help you prepare for the New SAT. If we covered every concept in Algebra I, Geometry, and Algebra II, this book would be at least 100 pages longer.

How Will this Book
Approach the Math Section?

In this section of the book, we will cover many math concepts that may appear on the test. You will learn how you already have great connections in your everyday life that will help you solve math problems. In addition, as I have previously mentioned, many school systems focus far too much on memorization. As a result, many of you may not have developed strong reasoning or logic skills. In this section, I will introduce you to several methods that will help you develop your logic and reasoning skills. We will also work on cutting down on careless errors and learn some new methods that will help you solve math problems in different ways than you may have learned in school.

Calculators

Before we get started on actual questions, let's talk about a very valuable asset: your calculator.

Dr. S. A. Tea: Okay, who feels completely helpless without a calculator?

Wictoria: Great Wizard of the SAT, I would be lost without my calculator. If I didn't have my calculator I would never know that two plus two is five.

Dr. S. A. Tea: Actually, Wictoria, two plus two is four.

Zino: Hey, hoser: That's why she needs a calculator, eh?

What Type of Calculator Can You Use on the SAT?

According to the College Board Web site, "You can use *almost any* four-function, scientific, or graphing calculator . . . "

Here are some exceptions that are listed on the College Board Web site:

- **Hand-held minicomputers or laptop computers**
- **Electronic writing pads or pen-input devices**
- **Pocket organizers (PDAs)**
- **Calculators with QWERTY (typewriter-like) keyboards**
- **Calculators with paper tape**
- **Calculators that "talk" or make unusual noises**
- **Calculators that require an electrical outlet**
- **Thermonuclear devices**
- **Your Dad**
- **Stephen Hawking**

(Okay, so we made up the last three exceptions.)

Dr. S. A. Tea's Tips for Calculators

Practice with the calculator you will use when you take the SAT.

1. Pick a calculator you have used before. For example, even if Texas Instruments releases a new scientific calculator that not only calculates logarithms and trigonometric functions, but also shoots three-point baskets and does the Macarena, be careful! If you don't feel comfortable with a calculator, your score may suffer. Make sure you practice with your calculator before you take the test.

2. You should try to use a scientific or graphing calculator on the New SAT. It is not necessary to use a scientific or graphing calculator on the Current SAT. However, the New SAT may have some questions that will be easier to solve with a more advanced calculator (for example, questions involving trigonometric functions, exponents, etc.).

3. Before you take the SAT, check with the College Board Web site to see if there has been any change in the calculator policy. It's possible that the College Board may disallow additional types of calculators in the future. It's always wise to look at the Web site information on calculators before you take the test.

Multiple-Choice and Student-Produced Responses Methods

The Math section has two question types: Multiple-Choice and Student-Produced Responses. The good news is that many of the techniques discussed in this section will apply to both question types.

Dr. S. A. Tea's General Tips for Doing Well on the Math Section

1. Learn to catch your careless errors. More often than not, you may find yourself missing seemingly easy questions on the Math section. If you can learn to avoid making simple errors on the SAT, you will find that your score will improve dramatically.

Catching your careless errors can have a huge effect on your score.

2. Don't limit yourself to one method. As I mentioned in the opening section of the book, many of you are constricted in school. Sure, you can use algebra to solve a problem, but often you can use other methods, such as taking advantage of the answer choices, or connecting math problems to real life. This isn't school. You can do things any way you would like. The most important thing is getting the correct answers.

3. Learn to avoid the tricks of the test. Learning to recognize the tricks of the test can turn a good score into a great one.

Careless Errors

Dr. S. A. Tea: Okay, let's talk about careless errors. Yes, Uhhhhh?

Uhhhhh: I made da careless error once.

Dr. S. A. Tea: Only once? Or does time just lump together for you?

Uhhhhh: Huhhhh? Anyway, da coach told me da best way to practice shootin' da ball was to practice in da dark.

Dr. S. A. Tea: I've heard about that technique. What went wrong? Did you trip in the gymnasium because you couldn't see?

Uhhhhh: Gymnasium? Oh, was dat wat the coach was talking about? I was in my parents' living room and I broke some of da furniture . . .

Dr. S. A. Tea: . . . What a surprise . . .

Uhhhhh: Huhhhh?

Dr. S. A. Tea: Never mind. Now for many of you, careless errors drastically reduce your scores. Here are some tips to help you cut down on careless errors.

Dr. S. A. Tea's Tips for Cutting Down on Careless Errors

1. Go slower. Hey, it may sound obvious, but if you simply take a little more time per question, you will find that you will continue to cut down on careless errors.

2. Go back to check your work over. If you would rather work the section quickly, make sure that you go back to look for careless errors. Take a few extra seconds and punch everything into the calculator again. Even if you discover a few mistakes, that could change your score substantially.

3. Write down notes on the test. For example, if you're solving an algebraic equation, take the extra few seconds to write neatly. Often students make mistakes merely because they misread their own handwriting.

Make Connections to Everyday Life

One way to handle math is to make connections to everyday life. Here we will take three basic concepts (averages, percentages, and fractions) and show you how you can make connections between each of these concepts and your own life. As you read each section, try each problem yourself before reading on.

Conversation with Thor about the "limbersome" gymnastic girls

Dr. S.A.Tea: Thor, I understand you are a big gymnastics fan.

Thor: Doctor Du-hude, for real, these chicks are so limbersome!

Dr. S.A.Tea, (thinking to himself): Limbersome, limbersome. (Out loud) Thor, do you mean they're limber?

Thor: Yeah, they're limbersome.

Dr. S.A.Tea: Thor, "limbersome" is not a word.

Thor: Come on, Doctor Du-hude, I say "awesome." It wouldn't make any sense if I said "awe."

Dr. S.A.Tea: Arggggggggh!

Use your own life to help you on the SAT.

Averages

Dr. S. A. Tea: First, let's take a simple problem involving averages:

What is the average of 4x and 6x?

A) 2*x*

B) 4*x*

C) 5*x*

D) 6*x*

E) 10*x*

Dr. S. A. Tea: Thor, what did you get for an answer?

Thor: Answer (A), uh, 2*x*?

Dr. S. A. Tea: What I want you to do, Thor, is to connect this question to your own culture. Let's make this one really visual. Instead of using *x*'s, let's turn this variable into something visual: GuessMonkeys. Now the problem looks like this:

What is the average of [monkeys] *and* [monkeys]?

A) 2 GuessMonkeys

B) 4 GuessMonkeys

C) 5 GuessMonkeys

D) 6 GuessMonkeys

E) 10 GuessMonkeys

Dr. S. A. Tea: Thor, another word for "average" is "middle," right?

Thor: Roight.

Dr. S. A. Tea: Still, you picked choice (A), 2. Do you still think that's correct?

Thor: Nooooo way, Doctor Du-hude. That's far too few GuessMonkeys.

Dr. S. A. Tea: Okay, well what would be the correct answer?

Thor: Answer (C), 5. The middle of 4 GuessMonkeys and 6 GuessMonkeys would be 5 GuessMonkeys. Five GuessMonkeys . . . That would be a lot of GuessMonkage!

Dr. S. A. Tea: GuessMonkage?

Zino, *sighing*: Thor is trying to say that there would be a lot of GuessMonkeys.

Dr. S. A. Tea, *to himself*: Zino is translating for Thor?

Percentages

Dr. S. A. Tea: Now let's move on to another concept: percentages. Here's a basic percentage question.

What's 90% of 20?

A) 9

B) 18

C) 90

D) 180

E) 1800

Dr. S. A. Tea: Wictoria, what answer did you pick for this question?

Wictoria: Answer (E), 1800.

Dr. S. A. Tea, *not looking surprised:* Wictoria, let's connect this problem to something you might deal with in real life. Let's say that you were watching *The Osbornes*.

Wictoria: I love that show! Kelly is my idol. The way she wears her hair and does her eyeliner is . . .

Dr. S. A. Tea, *cutting her off:* How fascinating. However, let's use Ozzy Osborne to help you solve this problem. Here's the rewording of the question using Ozzy Osborne:

If Ozzy Osborne speaks 20 sentences, and 90% of these sentences are unintelligible, how many sentences will be unclear?

A) 9

B) 18

C) 90

D) 180

E) 1800

Wictoria: Great Wizard of the SAT, oh, I see. *(Wictoria furiously starts punching numbers into her calculator.)* 1800 would be way too high. I forgot that when you calculate percentages, you have to move the decimal point two places to the left. I just multiplied 90×20. Instead, I should have multiplied $.9 \times 20$. The answer is (B), 18.

Dr. S. A. Tea: Witch is the correct answer.

Wictoria: Very funny.

Fractions

Dr. S. A. Tea: Okay, let's try one last simple category: fractions. Here's a basic fraction question:

There are two fractions: $\dfrac{10}{11}$ and $\dfrac{11}{12}$; which is bigger?

A) $\dfrac{10}{11}$

B) $\dfrac{11}{12}$

C) They're equal

D) Can't be determined

E) Why are we asking Uhhhhh?

Dr. S. A. Tea: Okay, let's go to the master of the SAT: Uhhhhh. What was your answer?

Uhhhhh, *approximating human thinking:* $\frac{10}{11}$.

Dr. S. A. Tea: Uhhhhh, let's look at this in a different way. Your main sport is basketball, right?

Uhhhhh: Yeah, I'm good at da basketball.

Dr. S. A. Tea: Okay. Anyway, do you have a higher free-throw percentage if you make 10 out of 11 free throws or 11 out of 12 free throws?

Uhhhhh: Dat's easy. Eleven out of 12 free throws. I made dat last free throw.

Dr. S. A. Tea: Right. So, what's bigger? $\frac{10}{11}$ or $\frac{11}{12}$?

Uhhhhh: $\frac{11}{12}$ . . . By da way, was answer (E) an insult?

Dr. S. A. Tea: Ah, progress.

You may feel that those problems were far too easy. They were. The purpose of presenting those problems was to show you how you should try to make connections between your everyday life and math. Okay, let's move on to some slightly more difficult problems.

Practice Exercises

Now it's your turn. Here are two problems in which making a connection to real life should make a difference for you. The answers and explanations follow the set of problems.

Pay attention, Du-hude!

1) A couple goes out for dinner and is charged $30 for food and $2.25 for tax. What amount of tax will they pay on a $20 meal?

A) $.15

B) $1.50

C) $2.50

D) $2.67

E) $15.00

2) A class of 10 students takes a test. The entire class scores an average of 78 on the test. The average of four of the students is 90. What is the average of the other students in the class?

A) 50

B) 70

C) 80

D) 85

E) 90

ANSWERS & EXPLANATIONS:

Problem #1

The answers on the test often parallel real-life situations, so stop and think about it . . . Would you pay only 15 cents in tax for a meal? Would you pay $15.00 in tax for a $20 meal? (If you picked $15.00 for an answer, you would be paying almost as much in tax as for the meal itself!)

Even if you just eliminate these two answers you have put yourself in significantly better shape. First, you need to determine the tax percentage. You can do this, by working with the numbers from the first meal.

$$\frac{2.25}{30} = ?$$

You should come up with .075, or 7.5%. (Remember, to change decimals into percentages, move the decimal two places to the right.)

At this point, all you have to do is multiply .075 × 20 and you will get the right answer of $1.50.

Answer (B) is the correct answer.

Problem #2

Let's look at the answers first:

A) 50

B) 70

C) 80

D) 85

E) 90

Before you calculate, think about if this situation occurred at school. If the average of an entire class is 78 and some of the students averaged 90, clearly the other students would have to average under 78 to balance out the numbers. For that reason, without doing any calculation, answers (C), (D), and (E) are wrong.

Here's how we will solve this problem:

First, let's get a total amount of points for all of the students in the class.

10 (number of students) × 78 (average) = 780

Next, let's determine the amount of points scored by the four students who averaged 90.

4 × 90 = 360

Now, let's subtract the second total from the first total.

780 − 360 = 420

Finally let's figure out the average for the remaining six students. (Remember that we started with 10 students and we have now accounted for the scores of 4 of the students. That leaves 6 students.)

$$\frac{420}{6} = 70$$

Answer (B) is the correct answer.

Conversation with Xasmine about going "chopping" with Zino

Dr. S.A.Tea: So, Xasmine, what are you going to do after school today?
Xasmine: Oh, Zino asked me to go "chopping" with him, but I am going to pick the mall.
Dr. S.A.Tea: Chopping?
Xasmine: Oh, you know that cute little accent he has. He's trying to say "shopping."
Dr. S.A.Tea: Actually, Xasmine, I hate to break it to you, but I think when Zino said "chopping," he actually meant chopping. He likes to go to the forest and chop down trees.
Xasmine: The forest? So ewww! Bugs, wild animals, no air conditioning. Will I go? Like no-ooh!

Time Cheating

Dr. S. A. Tea: Now, let's talk about a new concept: *Time Cheating*.

Xasmine: Oooh, like I've so been reading about that. Eee-yay-ee, who wants to grow old? Someday I am definitely going to have plastic surgery. Maybe I'll start with my eyes . . .

Dr. S. A. Tea, *cutting her off:* Xasmine, thanks for sharing, however what I want to talk about is how sometimes you can solve problems in a quicker way.

Sometimes there are quicker ways to solve problems. If something looks difficult, try to pull back from the problem. Try to avoid immediately diving into long calculations. Take a new look, maybe there's a shortcut.

Example:

If $n = \dfrac{7(a+b+c+d)}{4}$, then how can the average of a, b, c, and d be expressed in terms of n?

A) $7n$ B) $3n$ C) $\dfrac{n}{4}$ D) $\dfrac{n}{7}$ E) $\dfrac{n}{28}$

EXPLANATION:

This looks like a very difficult question. It seems like you are going to have to perform all kinds of difficult calculations, right? Wrong. The average of a, b, c, and d is:

$$\frac{a+b+c+d}{4}$$

Take another look at the question. All you have to do to get the correct answer is to move the "7" from the right-hand side of the equation to the left-hand side by dividing both sides by 7. Then the equation looks like this:

$$\frac{n}{7} = \frac{(a+b+c+d)}{4}$$

A) 7n B) 3n C) $\frac{n}{4}$ D) $\frac{n}{7}$ E) $\frac{n}{28}$

Now the answer should just jump out at you.

(D) is the correct answer.

Here's one to try on your own. There are many ways to solve this problem. See if you can find the quickest one.

Is there a quicker way?

A plumber charges a fixed price for a house call and an additional charge for each 15 minutes he has to work on a job. If he charges $80 for a 45-minute job and $100 for a 75-minute job, how long will he charge for a two-hour job?

If you're looking for me, I'll be on the planet Septicor.

A) 60

B) 65

C) 110

D) 130

E) 180

EXPLANATION:

You can do this problem a few different ways. Most people will try to determine the fixed price <u>and</u> the price per 15 minutes, thinking that knowing both prices is necessary to solve the question.

However, let's look at the problem this way. If the plumber charges $80 for a 45-minute job and $100 for a 75-minute job, he is charging $20 for the difference: 30 minutes. If you divide 20 by 2, you have the charge for each 15-minute interval: 10.

At this point all you have to do is determine how many 15-minute intervals there are between 75 minutes and 120 minutes (two hours).

$$120 - 75 = 45$$

Forty-five minutes can be broken up into three 15-minute intervals. If the plumber charges $100 for a 75-minute job, then he would charge $130 for a 120-minute job.

$$\$100 + 3(10) = 130$$

(D) is the correct answer.

Two Methods to help you with Multiple-Choice Math: Dude, Check Out Their Answers and Dude, Pick Your Own Numbers

Wictoria: Great Wizard of the SAT, I have a terrible time with math in school. Isn't there an easier way to do some of the problems without using algebra?

Dr. S. A. Tea: Why, yes, Wictoria, and thank you for asking. One of the common themes that run through this book is the idea that you can try out your own thoughts and you can check out the test maker's answers. Now we are going to see how you can adapt this method to help you with the Math section.

Dude, Check Out Their Answers:

We've already seen how for many of the other sections of the SAT you can use the Dude, Check Out Their Answers method. This method also works for math. Let's look at an example:

If the average of y and 3y is 12, then y =

A) 3

B) 6

C) 12

D) 15

E) 18

One of the five answers is right: why not check out the answers?

You could try to do this problem using algebra, but there's another way: *Dude, Check Out Their Answers*. First of all, we know one of these five answers is correct. The question asks, "What is *y*?" All we are going to do is substitute the different answers in for *y* until we find the answer that works with the whole problem.

Before we start with the method, let's discuss something important. If you look at the problem that we are discussing, you will notice that the answers are listed in ascending order. This is usually the case for the problems in the Math section of the SAT. As you will see shortly, this pattern will help you save time with the new methods you are about to learn.

Step 1: Start with the middle answer

Most people would start by checking the first answer (A), 3; however, there is a better reason to start with the *middle* answer (C), 12. If 12 fits correctly, it is the correct answer and you are done with the problem. If 12 is too big, answers (D) and (E) are also too big and can be automatically discarded. If 12 is too small, answers (A) and (B) are also too small and can be automatically eliminated. Therefore, by starting with the middle answer you can often eliminate three answers at once.

Let's start with the middle answer: 12. If you substitute 12 for y, the problem will read: The average of 12 and 36 (12×3) is 12. Does that make any sense to you? Is 12 halfway in between 12 and 36?

No. That means answer (C) is incorrect .

Step 2: If Answer (C) is incorrect, decide whether you need to move up or down. If you move up, try answer (D); if you move down, try answer (B).

Is answer (C) too big or too small? Well, clearly, if you substitute 15 for y you'll see that we will be going even further in the wrong direction. If you substitute 15 for y, then the question would read the average of 15 and 45 (3×15) is 12.

Obviously, we have to go the other way. Let's check answer (B). If you replace 6 for y, then the question reads: The average of 6 and 18 (3 × 6) is equal to 12. This is the correct answer since 12 is halfway between 6 and 18.

Answer (B) is the correct answer.

Practice Exercises

Now, it's your turn. Obviously you could try to solve these problems using algebra, but for now why don't you try using the Dude, Check Out Their Answers method. The first problem is a medium-level question, but the next question is a more difficult question: a question that students who score in the 600s and 700s in math often get wrong. (The answers and explanations to the answers follow below.)

1) If $6\sqrt{y} + 13 = 37$, **then** y =

A) 4

B) 9

C) 16

D) 25

E) 36

2) Out of 60 students in a room, the ratio of girls to boys is 4 to 6. How many girls are in the room?

A) 20

B) 24

C) 36

D) 40

E) 44

ANSWERS & EXPLANATIONS:

Problem #1

Step 1: Start with the middle answer.

If you start with answer (C), you will see that this choice is correct. Here is how you could have used the *Dude, Check Out Their Answers* method on this problem.

Plug in 16 (answer [C]) for *x*. The problem now reads:

$$6\sqrt{16} + 13 = 37.$$

Is that true? Yes. $6 \times 4 + 13 = 37$, or $24 + 13 = 37$. You have solved the problem.

Answer (C) is the correct answer.

Problem #2:

Step 1: Start with the middle answer

The question asks, "How many girls are in the room?" Start by plugging in answer (C) 36 for the amount of girls. If you look back at the first sentence, something should bother you immediately. According to the ratio, there are more boys than there are girls. However, if there were 36 girls, that would mean that there would only be 24 boys (60 − 36).

Step 2: If Answer (C) is incorrect, decide whether you need to move up or down. If you move up, try answer (D); if you move down, try answer (B).

Clearly, answers (C), (D), and (E) are all too high. Let's try answer (B). If you substitute in 24 for the amount of girls, that would leave 36 for the amount of boys (60 − 24). Then it is just a simple matter of comparing these numbers to the ratio in the problem.

Does $\dfrac{24}{36} = \dfrac{4}{6}$?

Yes. If you reduce $\dfrac{24}{36}$ you will see that it equals $\dfrac{4}{6}$.

Answer (B) is the correct answer.

Wictoria: Wow, Great Wizard of the SAT. This method makes math so much easier! But, I also have a lot of trouble with the problems that have x's and y's.

Uboreme: X's and y's, x's and y's. Why do they use this code? Why don't they tell you what's going on? I tell you, it's a government plot, man.

Xasmine: Ooooh, are you talking about *The X-Files*? That's such a cool show! Like I was so depressed when they pulled that off the air . . .

Dr. S. A. Tea, *cutting her off:* So, anyway, getting back to Wictoria's question, x's and y's are often used as variables. There's good news for you, Wictoria: Here's another method that will help you out with questions that involve variables.

Dude, Pick Your Own Numbers:

Let's look at another method that we will be able to use on both the Multiple-Choice questions and the Student-Produced Responses questions: the *Dude, Pick Your Own Numbers* method. The simplest way to demonstrate this method is to look at a problem.

Example:

If x = 5m, then the average of x and m =

A) *m*

B) 2*m*

C) 3*m*

D) 4*m*

E) 5*m*

This isn't school. No one will see your work. Try your own numbers.

The first question you may have is, Why not use the *Dude, Check Out Their Answers* method as we have before? The answer is very simple. The *Dude, Check Out Their Answers* is a great method, but it is sometimes difficult or even impossible to apply if there are variables (*x*'s, *y*'s, etc.) in either the answers or the questions. Thus, it's time for us to learn a new method: the *Dude, Pick Your Own Numbers* method.

Step 1: Pick your own numbers for the variables

What we're going to do is pick numbers for *x* and *m* that

make the first statement true and then just see what we end up with in the answers. Let's talk about picking numbers. You always want to make it easy on yourself, so generally you want to pick small positive integers. It might be a good idea to stay away from picking the number 1. You also don't want to pick the same numbers for different variables. (I will explain the reason for this later.)

Okay, ready? Let's try picking 2 for *m*. If you substitute 2 in for *m* in the first equation ($x = 5m$), then you will see that in this case *x* would be equal to 10. We will be labeling the numbers we picked above the variables, something I would suggest that you do whenever you use the *Dude, Pick Your Own Numbers* method.

Here's what your work should look like so far after making this first substitution:

　10　　2
If $x = 5m$, then the average of *x* and *m* =

Step 2: Work the problem through to find the numerical answer you would get by using the numbers you picked for the variables. (Make sure that once you pick a number for a variable, you use that same number in place of the variable all the way through the problem.)

Then, move to the second part of the sentence, "the average of *x* and *m*." Once you have picked numbers for your variables, use the same numbers each time you see those variables. In other words, in this case, since you have picked 10 for *x* and 2 for *m*, you should continue to substitute in those values every time you see *x* and *m*. Now the problem should look like this:

10   2   10   2

If $x = 5m$, then the average of x and m =

Step 3: Once you have determined a numerical answer, check the answers to find that same number.

First, let's answer the last part of the question using the numbers you selected. What is the average of 10 and 2?

The average of 10 and 2 is 6, so with the numbers you picked you are looking for an answer of 6.

Here, for some of you, there might be a problem. Obviously if you look at the answers, none of them looks like 6 at first glance.

A) m

B) $2m$

C) $3m$

D) $4m$

E) $5m$

However, what was the number you picked for m? 2, correct? Therefore when you look at the answers you have to sub in 2 every time you see m. Now, look at the answers.

A) 2

B) 2×2, or 4

C) 3×2, or 6

D) 4×2, or 8

E) 5×2, or 10

Therefore, **the correct answer is (C).** Still confused? Let's see how answer (C) would work for just about any pair of numbers that make the first equation, $x = 5m$, true.

Let's say this time you pick 15 for x and 3 for m. In this case, the average would be 9. If you substitute 3 in the answers every time you see m, you will see that (C) is the correct answer: $3 \times 3 = 9$

Practice Exercises

Now, here are two problems to do on your own. Once again the first problem is easier and the second one is more difficult. There are some hints under problem #1 to help you get started. The answers and explanations to the answers will be on the next page.

1) If j is the average of n and 8, and k is the average of n and 4, what is the average of j and k?

Let's help you get off to a good start. Try substituting in a simple number for *n* in problem #2 (perhaps 2 or 4 might be a good choice). Then it's like doing a math crossword puzzle. Once you know *n*, calculate *j* and *k*, etc. Remember, you have to use the same number for *n* in the answers that you used in the question.

A) 12

B) 6

C) $\dfrac{n+12}{4}$

D) $\dfrac{n+12}{2}$

E) $\dfrac{n+6}{2}$

2) *If the cost of x carrots is y cents, what is the cost in cents of z carrots at the same rate?*

A) xy

B) $\dfrac{xy}{z}$

C) $\dfrac{xz}{y}$

D) yz

E) $\dfrac{yz}{x}$

ANSWERS & EXPLANATIONS:

Problem #1

Step 1: Pick your own numbers for the variables

Let's say that you picked 2 for *n*, here's what the problem should look like:

If j is the average of n² and 8, and k is the average of n² and 4, what is the average of j and k?

Step 2: Work the problem through to find the numerical answer you would get by using the numbers you picked for the variables. Make sure that once you pick a number for a variable, you use that same number in place of the variable all the way through the problem.

If you do some quick calculations, you should be able to determine that j is 5 (the average of 2 and 8), and k is 3 (the average of 2 and 4). Next, you need to determine the average of j and k. Let's look at the end of the problem:

$$5 \qquad 3$$

. . . what is the average of j and k?

The average of 5 and 3 is 4. So now you are looking for an answer of 4.

Step 3: Once you have determined a numerical answer, check the answers to find that same number.

Look at the answers. At first glance there is no apparent answer of 4.

A) 12

B) 6

C) $\dfrac{n+12}{4}$

D) $\dfrac{n+12}{2}$

E) $\dfrac{n+6}{2}$

Obviously answers (A) and (B) are wrong. Neither answer is equal to 4. All you have to do now to get a correct answer is insert the value you picked for n, which was 2, into answers (C), (D), and (E), and see which one works out to be the answer of 4.

If you plug in 2 for *n* in answer (E), you can see that this is the right answer.

$$\frac{2+6}{2} = 4$$

Answer (E) is the correct answer.

Problem #2

Step 1: Pick your own numbers for the variables

Let's say that you had plugged in 2 for *x*, 4 for *y*, and 6 for *z*. Remember that you have to plug in numbers for all of the variables in the question. The question should now look like this:

2   4   6

*If the cost of **x** carrots is **y** cents, what is the cost of **z** carrots at the same rate?*

Step 2: Work the problem through to find the numerical answer you would get by using the numbers you picked for the variables. Make sure that once you pick a number for a variable, you use that same number in place of the variable all the way through the problem.

Let's put this into a real-life situation. If you went to a store and bought 2 carrots for 4 cents, what would 6 carrots cost at the same rate? 12 cents, correct? The math is straightforward: If 2 carrots cost 4 cents, then each carrot cost two cents. Therefore, if you are buying six carrots they would cost 12 cents (6×2).

Step 3: Once you have determined a numerical answer, check the answers to find that same number.

Now you are looking for an answer of 12. Let's look at our answers again.

A) xy

B) $\dfrac{xy}{z}$

C) $\dfrac{xz}{y}$

D) yz

Limbersome?

E) $\dfrac{yz}{x}$

Here's what the answers would look like if you replaced the numbers you picked for the variables:

A) $2 \times 4 = \mathbf{8}$

B) $\dfrac{2 \times 4}{6} = \dfrac{8}{6} = \dfrac{\mathbf{4}}{\mathbf{3}}$

C) $\dfrac{2 \times 6}{4} = \mathbf{3}$

D) $4 \times 6 = \mathbf{24}$

E) $\dfrac{4 \times 6}{2} = \mathbf{12}$

Answer (E) is the correct answer.

One Quick Warning About the "Dude, Pick Your Own Numbers" Method

At this point, I do want to mention the only drawback to the *Dude, Pick Your Own Numbers* method. Let's go back to a previous problem in this section:

If *j* is the average of *n* and 8, and *k* is the average of *n* and 4, what is the average of *j* and *k*?

A) 12   B) 6   C) $\dfrac{n+12}{4}$ D) $\dfrac{n+12}{2}$ E) $\dfrac{n+6}{2}$

Let's assume that you had picked 6 to substitute for *n*. Then *j* would be 7 (the average of 6 and 8), and *k* would be 5 (the average of 6 and 4). The average of *j* and *k* would therefore be 6.

Perhaps you can already see the problem. Answer (B) is 6 and if you replace 6 for *n*, answer (E) will also be 6. If you work the problem out algebraically you will see that the answer is (E). However, what should you do if you are using the *Dude, Pick Your Own Numbers* method on this question?

If you use the *Dude, Pick Your Own Numbers* method, always check all of the answers. If more than one answer works with the number plugged in, try again and pick a different number. Plugging in 6 for *n* gives two possible answers, but as we showed earlier, replacing *n* with 2 can yield only the correct answer, (E).

Dude, Pick Set Numbers

Once in a while, it might be advantageous to use a method that is very similar to the *Dude, Pick Your Own Numbers* method— the *Dude, Pick Set Numbers* method. The idea here is that depending on the problem there may be certain obvious numbers that you might want to pick. Here's a good example:

Example:

$4/5$, $16/5$, $64/5$, $256/5$

How can the above sequence be represented as a formula using y to represent the specific term number? In other words, since $4/5$ is the first term, in this case y would be 1. $16/5$ is the second term, so in this case y would be 2, etc.

A) $1/5 \times 2^y$

B) $3/5 \times y^4$

C) $1/5 \times y^4$

D) $1/5 \times 4^y$

E) $3/5 \times 4^y$

ANSWER & EXPLANATION:

Step 1: Pick a number for the variable

Sure, you could try any number, but why not make it easy

on yourself? Let's examine the first term, so let's make y = 1 and see what answer works.

Step 2: Check out their answers

Now all you have to do is substitute 1 in for y in the answers and check out which answer equals $^4/_5$.

A) $^1/_5 \times 2^1 = ^1/_5 \times 2 = ^2/_5$

B) $^3/_5 \times 1^4 = ^3/_5 \times 1 = ^3/_5$

C) $^1/_5 \times 1^4 = ^1/_5 \times 1 = ^1/_5$

D) $^1/_5 \times 4^1 = ^1/_5 \times 4 = ^4/_5$

E) $^3/_5 \times 4^1 = ^3/_5 \times 4 = ^{12}/_5$

Since we were looking for an answer of $^4/_5$, **answer (D) is the right answer.**

Difficult Math Problems:

Dr. S. A. Tea: Some of you have problems with difficult math problems. *(He looks at Uhhhhh.)* And then some of you have problems with everything . . .

Dr. S. A. Tea's Tips for Handling Difficult Math Questions

1. Look for a point of attack. Sometimes the key to solving a difficult problem is discovering where to begin.

2. Try to work out a plan for handling the problem. Especially if you are stronger in English than Math, try to work out what you need to do in words.

3. Take it one step at a time. Many students rush questions and end up making careless errors.

4. Be sure that you are answering the question. A problem, for example, may start off by describing a situation in *months*, while the actual question may ask for an answer in *years*. Just be careful.

Don't panic: There's always something you can do.

Practice Exercises

Here are two difficult math problems. Use the four-step method above to see if you can solve them:

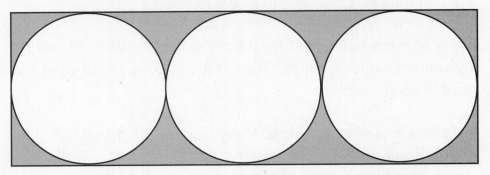

1) In the picture above, each circle has a radius of 3. Which answer is the best approximation of the area of the shaded region?

A) 15.5

B) 23.2

C) 31.3

D) 46.4

E) 51.5

2) A number z is greater than 0. $4x^2 + wx + 16 = (2x + z)^2$ for all values of x. What is the value of $w - z$?

A) 0

B) 4

C) 8

D) 12

E) 16

ANSWERS & EXPLANATIONS:

Problem #1

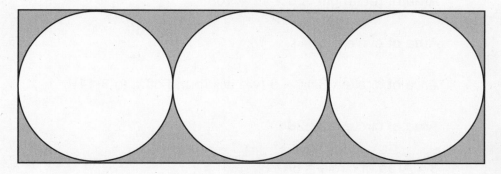

Step 1: Look for a point of attack.

Your first inclination will be to try to determine the area of the shaded portion. After all, that is what you are being asked to solve. However, if you step back and take another look you will see that it will actually be easier to try to determine the areas of the rectangle and circles first.

Step 2: Try to work out a plan for handling the problem.

    A. Determine the area of the rectangle

    B. Determine the area of each circle

    C. To find the area of the shaded portion, take the area of the rectangle and subtract 3 times the area of one circle.

Step 3: Take it one step at a time.

    Area of rectangle = Height × Base

If the radius of each circle is 3, then the diameter of each circle is 6, and the height of the rectangle is also 6.

If the diameter of each circle is 6 and the base of the rectangle is equal to the diameters of three circles, then the base of the rectangle is 18.

Area of rectangle is $6 \times 18 = 108$

Area of circle $= \pi r^2$

Area of circle $= 3.14 \times 9$ (we will round off π to 3.14)

Area of circle $= 28.26$

$3 \times$ Area of circle $= 84.78$

Step 4: Be sure that you are answering the question.

Remember again that the question is asking you for the area of the shaded portion of the figure. Go back to the formula you determined in step 2.

Area of rectangle $-$ 3(Area of 1 circle) $= 108 - 84.78 = 23.22$

The correct answer is (B)

Problem #2

First, let's look at the problem again.

A number z is greater than 0. $4x^2 + wx + 16 = (2x + z)^2$ for all values of x. What is the value of w − z?

Step 1: Look for a point of attack.

At first glance you may feel that this problem is a headache and your inclination may be to give up on trying to solve it. When you encounter a difficult problem like this, don't give up. Try to move things around and you will see an opening. Here, for example, why not use the foil method for the left-hand side of the equation. The problem will look like this:

$$4x^2 + wx + 16 = 4x^2 + 4zx + z^2$$

Now maybe you can see that you have $4x^2$ on both sides. After canceling out $4x^2$ on each side you have . . .

$$wx + 16 = 4zx + z^2$$

Step 2: Try to work out a plan for handling the problem.

After looking at this new equation, you will see how the two sides of the equation are roughly parallel to each other. Also, remember that z has to be positive. Now you can start to put together a plan to solve this problem.

A. Solve for z

B. Once you have the value of z, use this value to help solve for w

C. Subtract z from w

Step 3: Take it one step at a time.

A. Solve for z

If $z^2 = 16$, there are two possibilities for z: 4 or −4.

However, the problem states that *z* has to be positive. Therefore, *z* must be equal to 4.

   B. Solve for *w*

   Since $wx = 4zx$ and *z* is equal to 4, $wx = 16x$. Therefore, *w* must be equal to 16.

Step 4: Make sure that you are answering the question.

   Remember that the question is not asking you for the value of *z* or the value of *w*. The question is "What is the value of $w - z$?"

   Subtract *z* from *w*

   $16 - 4 = 12$

   (D) is the correct answer.

Avoiding Tricks

Dr. S. A. Tea: Let's talk about a key test-taking strategy: avoiding tricks.

Zino: Y'know, that gits me rat cheer **(pointing to his heart)**. Yesturdayee, Ah neerly got me keeled by a big Mack Triiiick.

Dr. S. A. Tea: Zino! We're talking about avoiding "tricks."

Zino: That's whut I say-ed, I avoidead a big Mac triiick.

Conversation with Zino about his accent

Dr. S.A.Tea: Zino, I have to ask you something that has been driving me crazy. I can't pin down your accent.
Zino: Well, my mutter was from Deutschland and my padre, he was-a from Italia. Then I have this Uncle, Vlad, who I vant to telllll you is a lettle scairry. He has a vairrrry pale face and dark hair and he alvays vears a cape. He vould come over late at night, ve'd never see him for breakfast or lunch . . .
Dr. S.A.Tea: Okay, okay, I think we get the point.

Dr. S. A. Tea's Tricks for Eliminating Tricks

1. Never worry about tricks if you know how to solve a problem. If you know how to solve a difficult question, go for it.

2. There are no tricks on easy questions. The purpose of an easy question is to make it *easy* to get right. Don't trip yourself up by worrying about tricks on easy questions

3. If you are trying to solve a difficult question and you're confused, consider eliminating the trick answers. If you learn to recognize the tricks, you might be able to eliminate answers on even the most difficult questions.

If you know the answer, don't worry about tricks. Go for it!

Here's an example of a difficult question. Before you look at the explanation, see if you can spot the tricks.

Example:

If n *is 20 percent greater than* p, *and* q *is 40 percent greater than* t, *then* nq *is what percent greater than* pt?

A) 40

B) 60

C) 68

D) 100

E) 200

(A), (B), and (D) are all tricks. Why? Some people are so lazy they pick 40 because it's in the question. Other people say, "20 + 40 = 60. . . . Hey, I'm a genius, I'll pick (B)." Some people would look at (D) and say, "100 percent . . . That's my favorite percentage."

The correct answer is (C). (You can work it out on your own.) The point is, who would pick (C) by guessing? *Sixty-eight* seems to have nothing to do with the two numbers in the problem: *20* and *40*.

Here's another difficult level question. See if you can eliminate the trick answers.

A train goes one way at 100 miles an hour and returns at 80 miles an hour to the same location along the same route. If the train has traveled for one hour, what is its average rate of speed to the nearest tenth of a mile?

A) 80

B) 88.9

C) 90

D) 95.7

E) 100

There are three obvious trick answers. (A) and (E) are trick answers because 80 and 100 appear in the problem. The biggest trick, however, is answer (C). Most people will pick this answer because they say that 90 is the average of 80 and 100. While that is true, that is not the question. The question asked for the average rate of speed for the trip. **The correct answer is (B).** (Again, you can work this out on your own.)

One final point: You could have had a chance to get this question right with a few basic thoughts. First of all, which way did the train go slower? Coming back, correct? Therefore, the train spent more time going 80 miles an hour. If the train had spent an equal amount of time going 80 miles an hour and 100 miles an hour, the answer would have been 90: the average of 80 and 100. However, if the train spent more time going 80 miles an hour, the average for the whole trip must be closer to 80 miles an hour. This means that you could eliminate answers (C), (D), and (E). You can eliminate (A) for one other reason. Answer (A) would only work if the train went 80 miles an hour for the whole trip. However, we know that the train went 100 miles an hour for a good part of the trip. Therefore, answer (B) must be correct.

Practice Exercises

Now, let's put it all together. Here are five multiple-choice math questions. The first two are easy level questions and the last three are more difficult. You may use any method you like. However, don't forget all of the great methods you have just learned!

When you do the last three problems, see if you can spot the tricks.

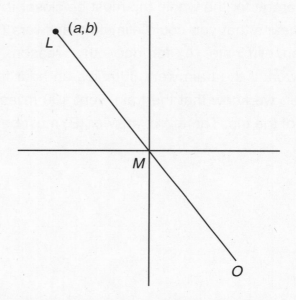

1) If in the figure above, LO is a line segment and LM = MO, what are O's coordinates?

A) $(-a, b)$

B) (b, a)

C) $(a, -b)$

D) $(-b, -a)$

E) $(-a, -b)$

2) If 2x + 7 = 18, then 2x − 7 =

A) 2

B) 4

C) 6

D) 7

E) 8

3) Bill has twice as many hats as Jim has. After Bill gives Jim 10 hats, Bill has 20 more hats than Jim does. How many hats did Bill have originally?

A) 40

B) 55

C) 60

D) 75

E) 80

4) At a store, a certain item is assigned a price on February 1st. Every month after that, the price is 20 percent less than the month before. If the price of the item was t dollars in February, what will be the price for the month of May (in the same year)?

A) .2*t*

B) .408*t*

C) .512*t*

D) .64t

E) .8t

5) On the first day of a sale, a store sold ¹/₃ of the TVs in the store. After the store sold 4 TVs on the second day, only ⁵/₉ of the original number of TVs remained. How many TV sets were in the store before the sale?

A) 20

B) 24

C) 36

D) 45

E) 50

ANSWERS & EXPLANATIONS:

Problem #1

Concentrate, man. Concentrate!

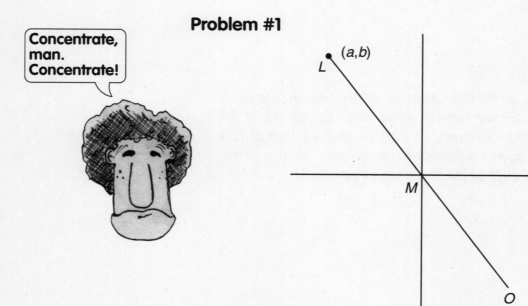

Point *L* is in a quadrant where the *y* coordinates will be positive and the *x* coordinates will be negative. Point *O* is in a quadrant that is completely opposite: the *y* coordinates will be negative and the *x* coordinates will be positive.

Since *LM* = *MO*, the coordinates of *O* will be exactly the negative version of *L*.

Since the coordinates of *L* are (*a*, *b*), the coordinates of *O* will be (−*a*, −*b*).

Answer (E) is the correct answer.

Ball, hoop.
Ball, hoop.

Problem #2

If 2x + 7 = 18, then 2x − 7 =

First, let's solve for *x*.

$$2x + 7 = 18$$

$$2x + 7 - 7 = 18 - 7$$

$$2x = 11$$

$$x = 5.5$$

Next, let's substitute 5.5 for *x* in the second equation.

$$2x - 7 =$$

$$2(5.5) - 7 =$$

$$11 - 7 = 4$$

Answer (B) is the correct answer.

Problem #3

Perhaps the easiest thing to do is to make a box out of the people and the events, and then use the *Dude, Check Out Their Answers* method.

	Bill	Jim
Before		
After		

The first thing to notice is the difference between using this method, and the method you would use in school. In school often you would make a box like this, but you would fill it with *x*'s and then try to solve the problem algebraically.

Step 1: Start with the middle answer

Instead, let's use our method and start filling in the box. If we start with answer (C), Bill would begin with 60 hats. If this is going to be the correct answer, everything else in the problem has to fit. In the first sentence it says Bill has twice as many hats as Jim. If answer (C) is correct, and Bill starts with 60 hats, Jim would have to start with 30. Your chart should now look like this:

	Bill	Jim
Before	60	30
After		

Look at the next sentence: Bill gives Jim 10 hats. Now your chart should look like this:

	Bill	Jim
Before	60	30
After	50	40

The third sentence of the problem clearly states that, after the transaction, Bill has 20 more hats than Jim. However, in this first chart there is only a difference of 10 between 50 and 40. This means answer (C) is incorrect.

Step 2: If Answer (C) is incorrect, decide whether you need to move up or down. If you move up, try answer (D); if you move down, try answer (B).

The next decision you need to make is whether to move up or down. You need to make the difference greater so it probably would be best to use higher numbers and look at answers (D) and (E).

When you examine answer (D), something should bother you immediately. If you divide 75 by 2 you get $37\frac{1}{2}$. Obviously you can't have half a hat and so now you know answer (D) is incorrect.

Let's look at answer (E). If you substitute 80 for Bill's starting point, the rest of the chart should look like this:

	Bill	Jim
Before	80	40
After	70	50

70 – 50 = 20. In other words, after Bill gives Jim 10 hats, there is now a difference of 20 hats. This is what you are looking for.

Answer (E) is the correct answer.

(Did you notice that answer (C) was the trick? Most people think about Jim gaining 10 hats and forget that Bill is also losing the 10 hats. This problem could also have been solved using algebra.)

Problem #4

Perhaps the easiest way to approach this problem is to use the *Dude, Pick Your Own Numbers* method.

Step 1: Pick your own numbers for the variables

There are many different numbers you could pick for *t*. However, the simplest one would be 100. Why? One hundred is a great number to pick for *t* because you are working with percentages.

Step 2: Work the problem through to see what numerical answer you would get by using the numbers you picked for the variables. Make sure that once you pick a number for a

variable, you use that same number in place of the variable all the way through the problem.

If you pick 100 for t, then that means that the price of the item is $100 in February.

In March, there is a 20% reduction. Since 20% of 100 is 20, that means the price of the item would now be reduced $20 and would now cost $80.

In April, the item is reduced another 20%. Since 20% of 80 is 16, that means the price of the item would now be reduced $16 and would now cost $64 (80 − 16).

Finally, in May, the item is reduced 20% one last time. Since 20% of 64 is 12.8, that means the price of the item would now be reduced $12.80 and would now cost $51.20 (64 − 12.80).

Step 3: Once you have determined a numerical answer, check the answers to find that same number.

If you look at the answers, none of the answers is 51.20.

A) $.2t$

B) $.408t$

C) $.512t$

D) $.64t$

E) $.8t$

That is because you are looking for an answer that is a fraction of the original number you picked for t. Since you picked

100 for *t*, answer (C) is the correct answer because 100 × .512 = 51.20.

> **Answer (C) is the correct answer.**

(Note that answers (B), (D), and (E) were all tricks. Answers (D) and (E) would be traps for someone who made the careless error of not going far enough in the months. Answer (B) would be a trap for someone who made the careless error of calculating the answer for one month beyond what the problem asked.)

Problem #5

This time you could use the *Dude, Check Out Their Answers* method.

Step 1: Start with the middle answer

Let's start with answer (C), the middle answer. Try to put this into a real life situation. Let's pretend that you work at Circuit City. Your store starts off with 36 TVs. The store sells $\frac{1}{3}$ of the TVs the first day. $\frac{1}{3}$ of 36 is 12. Therefore you now have 36 − 12 TVs left, or 24 TVs. On the second day, the store sells 4 more TVs. Now you have 20 TVs.

There's only one thing left to check: Is 20 TVs equal to $\frac{5}{9}$ of the original amount of TVs?

In other words:

$$\text{Is } \frac{20}{36} = \frac{5}{9}?$$

This statement is true, therefore:

Answer (C) is the correct answer.

(Notice also that answers (A), (B), and (E) could not have been correct because they are not divisible by 9.)

What's Your Score?

Okay, now let's total your score. Give yourself one point for every correct answer.

If you got . . .	
4 or 5 points	You are the Master of Multiple-Choice
2 or 3 points	You are not quite the Master of Multiple-Choice
0 or 1 point	When your math teacher mentions the word "number," he is referring to the condition of your brain

Student-Produced Responses

Dr. S. A. Tea: First, let's go through the directions for this section. On each *Student-Produced Responses* question, instead of picking from multiple-choice answers, you have to fill in your answer in a four-column grid. First of all, here is what the four-column grid looks like before it is filled in:

For example, if you thought the answer was 5/12, you would fill in the grid like this:

If you thought the answer was 3.75, you would fill in the grid like this:

The grid system also allows answers to be placed in different columns. For example, if you thought the answer was 231, you could fill in the grid like this:

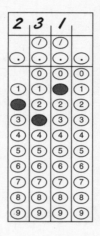

Hey, baby. Ketchup!

Or you could fill in the grid like this:

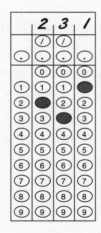

No, Zino! Wassup!

Similarly if the answer is 4, you could fill in the grid in these four ways:

Dr. S. A. Tea's Tip: Start with the First Column in the Grid

If the answer is a single digit number like 4, obviously you can fill in the grid four different ways as we just demonstrated. However, to save confusion, start with the column on the left and then use as many columns as you need.

In other words if the answer is 23, fill in the grid like this:

Dr. S. A. Tea's Tip: Be Careful When Filling in Mixed Numbers

One oddity of the test is that if you have a "mixed number" answer like $3\frac{1}{2}$, you must either grid this as 3.5 or $\frac{7}{2}$. Let's say on the other hand that you fill in the grid like this:

Unfortunately, the computer will read this answer as $\frac{31}{2}$. Here is one way the grid could be marked correctly.

Errors to Avoid on the Student-Produced Responses Section

Fill in the Columns

Dr. S. A. Tea: Now, let's go through a few basic errors that some of you made on the Student-Produced Responses section. Let's look at Uboreme's first answer.

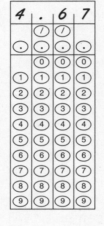

Dr. S. A. Tea: Uboreme, you did a great job to get the right answer, however you hurt yourself slightly when you wrote the answers in the space and then did not fill in the columns.

Uboreme: I'm an artist. I don't like to repeat myself.

Dr. S. A. Tea: I admire that attitude, but there's just one problem with that strategy on this section. You see, unfortunately, the computer only reads the filled in blanks in the columns.

Uboreme: That's so bourgeois.

(Dr. S. A. Tea looks at Uboreme and realizes that he is even stranger than he thought before.)

Dr. S. A. Tea: Okay, but here's how your answer should look.

Handwrite the answer, then fill in the grid.

Dr. S. A. Tea: Make sure that you handwrite your answer and fill in the grid.

There Are No Negative (or Minus) Quantity Answers

Dr. S. A. Tea: Let's move to the next situation. Thor, you seem to have entered new territory here.

Dr. S. A. Tea: You seem to have put negative answers on your answer sheet.

Thor: Doctor Du-hude, that's because I was feeling a negative vibe.

Dr. S. A. Tea: Yes, but as you can plainly see from the answer space for the Student-Produced Response area, there are no negative answers on this section.

Thor: Sorry, Doctor Du-hude. *(Putting his hand on his heart...)* From now on I will only emotiate positive energy and ergo positive answers on the Student-Produced Responses section.

Dr. S. A. Tea: Emotiate.... ? Er, thank you, Thor.

Proper Use of the Columns

Dr. S. A. Tea: Now, Wictoria, you seem to have another problem. For question #8, you came up with the answer *2.49,* which is the proper answer. You hand wrote the answers properly, the only problem is how you filled in the grid.

Dr. S. A. Tea: Wictoria, besides the fact that you are quite strange, why did you only use one column?

Wictoria: It's a waste of paper to use all four columns. Maybe if everyone who took the SAT only used one column we could save several trees a year!

Dr. S. A. Tea: Okay. . . . Do you understand, though, Wictoria, that if you put everything in one column the computer wouldn't know which order the numbers in your answer are supposed to be in?

Wictoria: Wow, Great Wizard of the SAT! I never thought of that.

Dr. S. A. Tea: Okay . . . Wictoria, saving the trees was a nice idea, but you need to use all four columns. Here is the proper way to fill it in:

Careful with Rounding Off

Dr. S. A. Tea: Uhhhhh, I have great news. Even though you didn't get the next problem right, you actually were close.

Conversation with Uhhhhh about college

Dr. S.A.Tea: Uhhhhh, aren't you worried about getting into college?
Uhhhhh: No. Da worst case I figure I can do what my mother does and go to the doctor.
Dr. S.A.Tea: Huh?
Uhhhhh: Every month my mother goes to the doctor to get college.
Dr. S.A.Tea: Doctor... college... Uhhhhh! Collagen. Your mother goes to the doctor to get collagen injections.
Uhhhhh: Yeah, she gets college.
Dr. S.A.Tea: Never mind.

Uhhhhh: What's da problem?

Dr. S. A. Tea: The only problem is that the answer was actually .333.

Uhhhhh: Dat's what I had originally, but I thought why use all de extra numbers and so I rounded down.

Dr. S. A. Tea: Conservation is great, Uhhhhh, but on this section when you have a repeating number you have to use all four columns in this section. Your answer should have looked like this:

Dr. S. A. Tea's Tip: Use the Dude, Pick Your Own Answers Method on the Student-Produced Responses Section

Obviously you cannot use the *Dude, Check Out Their Answers* method on this section. (There are no answers to check!) However, the *Dude, Pick Your Own Numbers* method can still be used on the Student-Produced Responses section. Here is a good example:

Why not try your own numbers?

Example:

In a certain country the population triples every 10 years. The population in the year $Y + 50$ will be how many times the population in the year Y?

Step 1: Pick your own numbers

Certainly you could attempt to do this question by setting up an equation. But why not just plug in numbers and see what happens? For example, let's set $Y = 0$. Then the problem reads:

In a certain country the population triples every 10 years. The population in the year 50 will be how many times the population in the year 0?

Step 2: Work the problem through with the numbers you have picked.

Now let's pick a starting point for the population. Let's use the simplest example and say that the population starts off with one person. Here's a chart of what happens:

Year	Population
0	1
10	3
20	9
30	27
40	81
50	243

After 50 years there are now 243 times the amount of people we started with. But, what would have happened if you had started off with a different population? If, for example, you had started with a population of 2, you would have ended up with 486. However, if you divide 2 into 486 you will still have 243. In fact, no matter what population you pick for a starting point, you will always end up with 243 times the amount of people you started with.

So the correct answer for the problem is 243.

Practice Exercises

Here are five Student-Produced Responses questions to try. The answers and explanations follow. Use the grids on this page to practice filling in the grid format.

1.

2.

3.

4.

5.

1) 3x = 12 − x, what is the value of x?

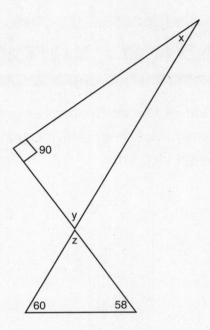

2) In the above triangle, what is the value of angle x in degrees?

3) For all numbers x and y, let x * y = 2x − 3y. What is 3 * 2 ?

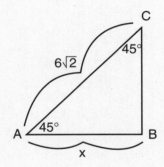

4) In the above triangle, if $\overline{AC}$ is $6\sqrt{2}$ and the angles are as marked, what is the length of x?

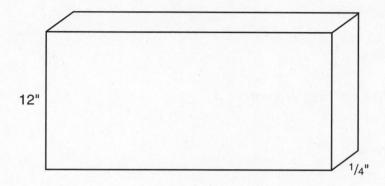

12"

1/4"

5) The height of the rectangular solid shown is 12 inches and its depth is 1/4 inch. The volume of the solid is 60 cubic inches. What is the width of the solid?

6) The Pesky Fly doubles its population every 10 minutes. After 60 minutes, how many times the original population of Pesky Flies will there be?

ANSWERS & EXPLANATIONS:

Problem #1

Here's the question:

3x = 12 – x, what is x?

The most important thing on this question is to take your time and make sure that you don't make a careless error.

First, let's move the *x* from the right side of the equation to the left side. This way we can have all the *x*'s on one side and all the numbers on the other side.

3*x* + *x* = 12 – *x* + *x*

Conversation with Uboreme about the true purpose of the SAT

Dr. S.A.Tea: Uboreme, I understand that you have a theory about the SAT.
Uboreme: Yeah, SAT man. The SAT is an evil government plot!
Dr. S.A.Tea: And what is the purpose of this plot?
Uboreme, checking over both shoulders to make sure no one is listening: You're never going to believe this: They're trying to get us to learn!
Dr. S.A.Tea, to himself: It's not working, is it?

$4x = 12$

$x = 3$

The correct answer is 3

Problem #2

Let's look at the picture again.

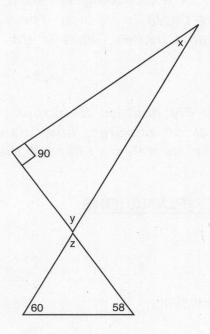

This is not a difficult problem. The crucial point is to take your time working through the steps and to be sure that you don't make any careless errors.

There are 180 degrees in a triangle. Therefore $180 - 60 - 58 = z$

$z = 62$

$y = z$ because they are opposite angles; therefore, y is also 62

We now know two of the angles in the top triangle. y is 62 and also there is a perpendicular angle, which has a value of 90. Therefore $x = 180 - 90 - 62$

$x = 28$

The correct answer is 28

Problem #3

First, don't panic. The test makers are just throwing a new symbol at you to see if you can handle it. This is robot work. All you have to do is substitute in the numbers in the proper place and you are all set.

Still watching you, du-hude.

If you look at how things line up, 3 matches up with x, and 2 matches up with y.

Therefore all you have to do is substitute in 3 for x in the equation, and 2 for y.

$2(3) - 3(2) = 0$

The correct answer is 0

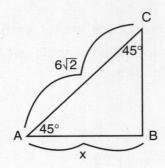

Problem #4

This problem can be solved one of two ways. One way is to find the length of $\overline{AB}$ by using trigonometry. In this case: Sin $45° = \frac{x}{6}\sqrt{2}$.

The second way to determine the length of $\overline{AB}$ is by remembering that in a 45-45-90 triangle, each of the smaller sides of the triangle has a $1:\sqrt{2}$ relationship with the hypotenuse. Therefore, since the hypotenuse is $6\sqrt{2}$ . . .

The correct answer is 6

Problem #5

1. First, think about the formula for volume of a rectangular solid:

Height × Width × Depth = Volume

2. You already have three pieces of the equation — fill them in.

$$12 \times \text{Width} \times \frac{1}{4} = 60$$

3. Simplify this and you have:

$$3 \times \text{Width} = 60$$

4. Therefore the Width is 20.

The correct answer is 20

Problem #6

The Pesky Fly doubles its population every 10 minutes. After 60 minutes, how many times the original population of Pesky Flies will there be?

Step 1: Pick your own numbers

Let's say that the Pesky Fly population starts off with 1 fly.

Step 2: Work the problem through with the numbers you have picked.

After 10 minutes there will be 2 flies, after 20 minutes there will be 4 flies, etc. Here is the chart for the rest of the time:

Minutes	No. of Flies
0	1
10	2
20	4
30	8
40	16
50	32
60	64

After 60 minutes, there will be 64 times the number of Pesky Flies you started with.

The correct answer is 64

What's Your Score?

Okay, now let's total your score. Give yourself one point for every right answer.

If you got . . .

4 – 6 points   **You are the Master of the Student-Produced Responses**

2 or 3 points   **You are not quite the Master of the Student-Produced Responses**

0 or 1 point   **PLEASE, don't ever work at a bank.**

Additional Math Problems

In the coming months, we will be developing some new math problems in a continuing effort to help you with the Math portion of the New SAT. Check the REA.com site every few weeks so that you can start working on these problems as soon as they are posted.

You're Done!

Congratulations! You have now finished the Math section of the book. Next up, the Conclusion.

Conclusion 5

Congratulations! You have now made it through the most difficult part of the book. Now we will discuss a few more simple tips:

A. How to sign up for a test

B. What you need to have with you on the day of the test

C. How to continue practicing after you have finished this book

Signing up for the Test

Your Choices for Signing Up:

A) If you're behind the times: Fill out the SAT form and send it by regular mail

B) If you're in tune with the times: Go to *Collegeboard.com* and sign up online

C) If you're a major slug: Go to the test site on the day of the test and do what's known as a "walk-in." (Essentially you just show up the day of the test and pay a higher fee for the privilege.)

D) If you're slightly psychotic: Fly to New York, go to the College Board office, knock on the door, and ask for Gaston Caperton, the president of the College Board. Tell Gaston that he shouldn't forget to put you down for the March 2005 test.

What Extras Do You Want to Pay for?

A) Either the *Student Answer Service* or the *Student Question and Answer Service*. For most test dates, the *Student Answer Service* is available and occasionally the *Student Question*

and Answer Service is available. You want to order the service that is available for your test date. It is important to order one of these services every time you take a test because you will then have a much more complete picture of your total test.

B) Rushing the Scores. Only do this when you are a senior and you need to know your scores immediately so you can decide if you need to take the test again.

C) Chrome Wheels. Oh, wait . . . we were talking about extras for the SAT.

Day of Test

Things to bring to the test

1. **A watch**

2. **Several no. 2 pencils**

3. **Photo ID**

4. **Your calculator**

5. **Admission ticket for the test**

6. **Water and a small snack**

You may be wondering . . .

Why do you want to bring a watch?

A) There may not be a clock in the room where you take the test.

B) There may be a clock in the room where you take the test but the clock may not work.

C) The school may have been built before clocks were invented.

D) It's hard to concentrate when you are mentally counting to 1500 (25 minutes × 60).

E) You have an expensive watch that tells you the time all over the world, and you are one of those people who just has to know what time it is in Borneo.

Why do you want to bring several pencils?

A) You're so spastic you will snap all of your pencils.

B) You can drive the student in front of you crazy by poking him continuously with one of your extra pencils.

C) You can do the annoying twirly pencil thing with both hands.

D) You can put the erasers of all your pencils together on the desk and make a teepee.

E) You can stick pencils in both of your ears, foam at the mouth, and get the College Board to cancel your test.

During the test, if you find yourself hyperventilating, what should you do?

A) Keep hyperventilating and discover Nirvana.

B) Stop and take 10 seconds of deep breaths. This will either return you to normal breathing or you will die (50–50 shot).

C) Try to hyperventilate even louder; maybe you can annoy everyone else enough so that they score poorly, too.

D) Try singing. Maybe you will sound like Alanis Morissette.

E) Try hypoventilating — whatever that is — to even out the effect.

Why do you want to bring water and a snack?

A) The New SAT is so long that they're considering making an "SAT Survivor."

B) There are no (B), (C), (D), or (E) choices. Answer (A) was funny enough on its own.

(Seriously, bring along water and a snack; however, it is possible that the proctor may not allow you to bring anything into the test. It's always worth a shot, though.)

Keep practicing!

What Can You Do Beyond this Book to Help Study for the New SAT?

Overall

The College Board has stated that it will release a book of practice SATs for the New SAT sometime in 2004. In the meantime, here are two books that would be useful for those students seeking extensive review and practice:

1. Ten Real SATs by the College Board. This is a book of 10 actual previously administered SATs using the Current SAT format. Obviously, it is great to practice with the actual tests. The main drawback to this book is that it does not have explanations for the answers.

2. The Very Best Coaching & Study Course for the SAT by REA. This book features six full-length tests using the Current SAT format. As is characteristic of REA's test preps, detailed explanations are provided — a factor that should help you improve your scores. Buy it at REA.com.

Improving Your Writing Skills

The best thing you can do to improve your writing skills is to write. It may sound simple, but the more you write, the more you will discover your style and fix any weaknesses. This is a time-honored principle that, as we said earlier, will reap rewards far beyond the SAT itself.

Take pride in your writing. Always endeavor to say things in an original way, and never settle for clumsy sentences or phrasing.

Improving Your Math Skills

Seek out math in your daily life. If you play baseball, figure out your batting average in your head. If you are shopping for clothes, estimate how much a discount will lower the cost of your purchase. If you are shopping for groceries with your family, look at the cost of each item and try to guess the total bill.

By all means use calculators, but try to spend some time every day making calculations in your own head.

Improving Your Reading Skills

There are essentially three groups of people:

1. Those who like to read.

2. Those who like to read but feel that they don't have enough time.

3. Those who hate to read.

If you're a person who likes to read, that's great! Just make sure that you save time to read every day. Over time, try to read more challenging books so that you can handle the more difficult reading passages on the test.

If you're a person who likes to read, but you feel that you are too busy, consider reading right before you go to sleep. Even if you can find time to read for a few minutes a day, those few minutes will change your SAT score.

If you're a person who hates to read, examine why you don't like reading. Maybe you dislike the books you're assigned in English classes at school: Is the subject matter unappealing to you? Well, guess what? You're on your own now. You can read anything you want. If you like sports, why not read sports biographies? Maybe your passion is fashion: Why not start reading fashion magazines? Do you have a favorite movie? Why not read the book it was based on?

Improving Your Vocabulary

As I mentioned in the introduction, my vocabulary changed drastically in high school after I worked with a list of 3,500 words in an attempt to change my SAT I verbal score. For me, this experience started a lifelong interest in vocabulary.

However, since the New SAT will drop the Analogies section and the emphasis in the New SAT will be more on reading and less on vocabulary, it's clearly no longer valuable to memorize huge lists of words that may or may not be on the New SAT. Does that mean that having a good vocabulary will not be important for success on the New SAT? No! I think what is far more important is developing a good feel for roots and prefixes, as well as learning how to make proper associations so that you actually retain the vocabulary words you study.

For example, if you are learning the word *belligerent*, why just memorize the definition: "aggressive"? Why not focus on the main root, *bell*, and then realize that almost all other words that contain the root *bell* will also be words that have to do with aggression. For example, the words *bellicose* and *antebellum* are both related to the word *belligerent* because they share the *bell* root.

If you are learning the word *wily,* why just try to memorize the definition: "tricky"? Instead, think about the obvious association: the cartoon character, Wile E. Coyote. Wile E. Coyote earned his name because he was always trying to trick the Road-runner.

Here are two books that I would recommend to improve your vocabulary:

1. The REA Interactive Flashcards® SAT Vocabulary Builder

2. Merriam Webster's Vocabulary Builder

The Incapables Say Goodbye

Well, the gang would like to say goodbye and wish you well.

Don't worry du-hude . . . You'll knock them wooscious! How
well will you do on the New SAT? Very.

So, like, do you want to go shopping with me after the SAT?

What's the XLK?

Dr. S. A. Tea: Oh, boy . . . those aren't even the letters of the SAT . . .

Here's what you do . . . You take your SAT answer sheet and you send it to the IRS. That's the only way to stop this government plot!

I'll be chanting for you.

Don't wurry, you da bum!

No, Zino! You're da bomb!

Index